But
GOD

But GOD

Hope
That
Never
Fails

VERNAE COFFEE

XULON PRESS

Xulon Press
2301 Lucien Way #415
Maitland, FL 32751
407.339.4217
www.xulonpress.com

© 2024 by Vernae Coffee

All rights reserved solely by the author. The author guarantees all contents are original and do not infringe upon the legal rights of any other person or work. No part of this book may be reproduced in any form without the permission of the author.

Due to the changing nature of the Internet, if there are any web addresses, links, or URLs included in this manuscript, these may have been altered and may no longer be accessible. The views and opinions shared in this book belong solely to the author and do not necessarily reflect those of the publisher. The publisher therefore disclaims responsibility for the views or opinions expressed within the work.

Unless otherwise indicated, Scripture quotations taken from the Holy Bible, New International Version (NIV). Copyright © 1973, 1978, 1984, 2011 by Biblica, Inc.™. Used by permission. All rights reserved.

Paperback ISBN-13: 978-1-66286-699-9
eBook ISBN-13: 978-1-66286-700-2

In Loving Memory

of my father, Sylvester Williams, mother, Vernie Warren Williams, grandparents, Flozell and Donzell Warren, Bill and Jennie Mae Williams & brothers, First Sargeant Lesly Williams, Navy Veteran Elvester Williams, and a special nephew and niece.

In Special Memory

of Maya, Joshua, and Caleb—my never forgotten Blessings.

In Appreciation

of my stepmother, Barbara Williams, and my aunts and uncles who were examples of faith, work ethic, and perseverance.

Acknowledgements

All honor and praise to God for breathing life into the words on these pages. May He be glorified by this collection.

Thank you to my husband and friend, Gossnar, who was my biggest encourager, along with my three children, David (his wife, Jennifer), Jenae, Chantel, and stepdaughter Ayriel (husband, Dashawn).

I also thank my ex-husband, David Matikke of Cameroon, Africa, who began this book journey with me, and is father of our three adult children, David, Jenae, and Chantel.

Blessings to my seven grandchildren, and those yet to be born. May you come to know, love, and walk with Jesus.

Thank you to Sardis Baptist Church of Birmingham, Ala. and Hunter Hill Baptist Church of Atlanta Ga. where my personal relationship with Christ took root.

Thank you to World Outreach Church, Schrader Lane Church of Christ, Lakeshore Christian, Strong Tower Bible Church, and Mount Zion Baptist Church of Middle Tennessee whose leadership and members were key in my survival and growth as a Christ Follower for over three decades.

Thank you to every teacher I've had from Kindergarten to 12th grade. I honor you.

Thank you to the Glenn High School Administration, Faculty, and Graduating Class of 1980. I remember and treasure you.

Thank you to Berea College and ETSU faculty, staff, and students who deepened my enthusiasm for serving others, lifelong learning, and work ethic.

Thank you to all the angels— Prayer partners, sibling, family members, men and women of faith, Poetry Live students, Left to Write Poetry Group—God sent along the way to encourage me to complete this project.

A special thanks to each person who contributed by writing a comment to accompany each poem and scripture. You are greatly appreciated.

A sunray of gratitude to McKayla Anne Rockwell, who dedicated a year of her life to stretching me as a poet and becoming a friend along the way.

> *"Be exalted, O God, above the heavens;*
> *let Your glory be over all the earth."*

Psalm 57:11

TABLE OF CONTENTS

LOVE, LOSS, AND LIFE 1
Butterflies in the Watermelon Patch 3
Echo 7
Restless Floors 8
But God 10
I Take Me Back 12
Daddy was More Than He was Not 14
Healing Feathers 19
My Next Breath 21
Invasion 23
Big Mama's Dumplings 26
Journey to the Diagnosis 29
Night Lights 36
Bereft 37
She Remembers 39
My Pecan Tree and Me 41
Mothers 43
A Life of Forgiveness 45
Her Reason to Live 47
Half-truth, Half-apology 49
Pride's Death 51
Woman of Soft Strength 54
That Day 57
It Is Not 59
Death Hurries Me 60
Distractions 62

But GOD | ix

Little World Changed Forever 64

Growth 66

Time to Smile Again 67

Soul Mate 69

Snapshots from Childhood 71

Missing You 73

True Love 75

First Vacation 77

Morning. 79

Freedom 81

I Thought You Would Come to Me. 83

Just Because 85

Break Me, Mold Me, Make Me Yours 87

You Are Not My Enemy 90

See Me 93

We Never Told Anyone. 95

See Me!. 97

If Acorns Were Cash 99

Comparti Allegria 101

Hold On! 102

Respect for the Blue 105

I Got Game 107

Dad Told Us 109

Childhood Fear 111

Food Addiction 113

Freedom Cost 115

Chosen 117

I See You. 119

A Lie 121

No Words Necessary. 122

x | *But GOD*

Promises Made 124

Daddy's Prints. 126

Ditch Digger 128

Hollow Throne 130

Why Should I?. 132

Becoming 134

Visit From an Angel 136

Choose Me 138

Thank You for the Dance 140

Just One. 142

Loved You. 144

Come to Me My Daughters 145

Barefoot Republic Camp. 147

Pseudo Friends 149

Today I Started Letting Go 150

School. 152

Summers at Big Momma's and Granddaddy's 154

The Bus Ride (Part I) 156

The Bus Ride (Part II). 158

The Bus Ride (Part III) 160

REDEMPTION. 163

He Calls. 165

Wounded Body 167

The Unseen Battle. 169

Surrendered. 172

Squealing Like an African Cicada 174

Nothing Yet Everything 176

More Faithful 178

WildFire 180

But GOD | xi

Don't Forget to Flush 182

I Believe YOU 184

The Cross 186

Worship Him 188

The WHO 189

Beyond Sunday Morning Greetings 191

What Is the Story of Your Brokenness 193

Forgiven 195

Love Covers 196

What a Joy 198

The Great "I AM" 200

Comfort less 202

In Every Moment 203

Worship Thee 205

Be Still and Know 207

The Answer 209

Words from my Barber 211

The Walk 213

BONUS POEMS FOR YOUR PRESCHOOLER 215

If I Were Real 217

Teddy Wet My Bed 219

Where Are Your Manners? 221

Bubbles 222

Just Being Me 223

Kind Lady 225

Thank You! 227

Butterfly 229

Momma Said 230

Poor Fly 231

xii | *But GOD*

Where's My Lunch? 232

Sleepy Time 234

Mother's Love. 235

Toddler's Response to Seeing Newborn Baby Sister 237

No 239

Jesus Watches Over Me 241

Sleep Training. 242

Time to Rise . . . . 244+

But GOD | xiii

LOVE, LOSS, AND LIFE

BUTTERFLIES IN THE
WATERMELON PATCH

have pursued me longer
than hums from my mother's vintage sewing machine,
first heard from her womb.
Their flutters vibrate above the voice in my head
touting uninvited thoughts—
you pray God did not hear.

When exploring my grandparent's watermelon patch,
   I floundered
     down an unfamiliar trail.
  Frolicking with bumblebees in black-eyed susie attire.
     They danced about me
       before stabbing
        shoulders,
         forearms,
          and cheeks.
A summer azure suddenly appears, mud-puddling on my arm—
softening the stingers, stuck like blue bubblegum on my shoe-bottom
beneath a sweltering day in June.
As I endured the crawl between sugar baby melons,
clay-like patches attach to my skin.
The dull finish conjured Momma's face in Fall of 1967
when my four siblings and I clung
to her 23-year-old still body—
the arms that hugged our tears.
   A roost of iridescent pieridae encircled Momma's
   head that day.

But GOD | 3

I maneuver through more giant leaves and melons.
Sun-dried manure grazes my shriveled knees.
The scent sizzles like the blood-coated metal that rav-
aged my brother's body,
leaving him hemorrhaging on a residential street
in Georgia.
    I glimpse a golden-yellow cloudless sulphur on the
    EMT's back
    as they hasten my brother away.   He would rise
    and flutter
    figure eights once again.

I struggle to nudge the largest sugar baby.
Its bulk more burdensome than the memory
of my father's broad shoulders
carrying his mother's cedar casket—still a boy.
Enchanted by a blue morpho on his hand that lightened his load,
    as he would mine on many of his tomorrows.

    Then I stumble
        upon
           a cracked melon frothing
like moon-shine vapors, permeating
my grandfather's flesh.
The odor consumes like the neighbor's septic tank backup—
a family of gray-banded hairstreak didn't mind. They winged
above my head with the resilience of my father's father.

Black seeds ooze through fizz,
sticking to the outer rind like the word nigger
labored to bond to me in high school
as I hurried home from work one Birmingham evening.
Eastern tiger swallowtails were my escorts.   That word never
caught me—

4 | *But GOD*

I bolt to fresher melons in pursuit of crisp air. Paralyzed
by the cancerous abyss in my friend's eyes as she gasps—
a monarch, wings constricted, perches atop her brow. She takes
her final breath,
her final bow. Our bond was sealed as her grip released mine.

Catnapping in the watermelon patch, I am awakened
by a blistering sun blasting like door-pounds
from the military chaplain and detective. I collapse
    before the words live,
        "Your brother and two-year old niece are no more".
But two painted ladies came lifting his wife and son from the flames.

Silence falls over the watermelon patch,
reminding me of those never-heard words
"I love you mommy" from my   unknown children
(who I know fly with the butterflies).
The hush confines more than Big Mama's corset—

My grandparent's watermelon patch is now overrun
with weeds, dead seeds, and dirt.
I no longer cavort with bees, but I have danced with pain.
It now follows more than leads—
And the butterflies still flutter…

"Therefore we do not lose heart. Though outwardly we are wasting away, yet inwardly we are being renewed day by day. For our light and momentary troubles are achieving for us an eternal glory that far outweighs them all. **18** So we fix our eyes not on what is seen, but on what is unseen, since what is seen is temporary, but what is unseen is eternal."

2 Corinthians 4:16-17

"Only in those moments when we approach the threshold of our own mortality's door do we have clear vision of those we have loved and loss in life."

—Jean E. W. Hill
Poet, Writer, Artist

Echo

You stepped into my palace,
and mistook it for a shack.

We strolled under dazzling stars—
but you only saw the dark.

I offered you my sapphire,
you tossed it like a river stone.

I imparted the gift of friendship—
You stepped forward with open palm.

"Then Caleb silenced the people before Moses and said, 'We should go up and take possession of the land, for we can certainly do it.' But the men who had gone up with him said, 'We can't attack those people, they are stronger than we are.'"

Numbers 13:30-31

"While people's perceptions of their world vary, some of us choose to see through a negative lens. We have a choice to view our world with light, love, and splendor. If you have a choice, why not see gold within sunrays instead of possible sunburn?"

—Jessica Tiara Beasley
Structural Engineer

RESTLESS FLOORS

Few things cause my father's footing to flinch.
Floor-boards   thump   thump   thump   as Dad drudges
his size 10's
from bed to bathroom and hallway to den.

    Lying a level beneath him, my rest, too, rides resistance,
    facing off with walls festooned with answerless questions—
    How can I do all of this? Care for Dad?
        My family?
        The business?

Dad's defibrillator taunts him from the depths of his chest wall
"You don't trust me to keep you alive if you fall   into sleep? Do you?"

    My spine to floor, eyes to ceiling, Dad's silhouette reappearing
    in the windows, awaking me to a weary advent of words that
    never slept—
    Should Dad move in with us? Or should we relocate?

He curses his decision to have the surgery,
then gives God thanks that he survived it.

    Light creeps down the stairs from the open bathroom door,
    echoing, "Your Dad will know the truth about your marriage
    if he comes to live with you—no protecting him anymore."

I mask up and diffuse lavender oil for a drop of sleep,
chasing it like the answers I seek to questions that paint each room.

I inhale, deeply poised for what I must embrace,
like the wind's gentle breath sways the leaves of trees outside Dad's home
back   and   forth   back   and   forth
back   and   forth.
        Our lethargy leans   into another morning.

8 | *But GOD*

"Truly my soul finds rest in God; my salvation comes from him."

Psalm 62:1

"In all of life's truly difficult questions, we are guaranteed no answers. Instead, we hear, 'Wait,' 'Listen,' and 'Watch.' We must choose each day to trust God's promises and that His mercy is enough for each day and new each morning. Only trust Him."

—Jeremy W. Anderson, OD

But God

I was the house across the street with a horizonal crack—
the one with fallen shutters that people point
to and laugh. The fissures in my asphalt driveway
were too damaged to be repaired.
But God permanently sealed my fractures
that I might be   *undeservedly*   spared.
I wore broken-down steps that visitors avoid,
fearing twisted ankle, broken foot,
or backward stumble into the yard.
But God launched angels to eliminate loose debris,
chisel and smooth away   rough edges in me, refilling deep faults
only He could see.
My brass doorbell had lost its voice
But God still heard my call, like the tea kettle's whistle
from the stove   down that hall.
My sofa's sunken cushions would grab, bite, and sting,
so most preferred to stand.
But God made it a place of prayer—
come closer you'll see elbow prints embedded there.
My washing machine shook like an earthquake,
causing all nearby   to pause.
But God was my strong tower when walls began to fall.
My electrical outlets were expired, dangling, strangled by its wire.
But God empowered my receptacles
with Holy Spirit fire.
Even my red and white oak strip floors were dented,
scratched, and caving in   until hidden chambers opened to
Jesus (Yeshua)—
and He proclaimed   me more   than my sin.
I am now the chateau on the hill
that many aspire to be. Drivers back up traffic

for kilometers to get a glimpse of me. My cedar doors
are two inches thick, and my ceiling kisses the sky. My crystal chandeliers
mesmerize those strolling by. But God still permits
my cedar doors to creak, and my oak porcelain tiles to crack
that never shall I forget, from whence comes my strength

"But God is so rich in mercy, and he loved us so much, that even though we were dead because of our sins, he gave us life when he raised Christ from the dead. It is only by God's grace that you have been saved."

Ephesians 2:4-5

"It is a spiritual dilemma… how Christ-followers are proclaimed 100 percent righteous according to scripture, and 100 percent of the time battling with fleshly and selfish desires. Honestly, we are constantly battling the internal war of the flesh versus the Spirit. The apostle Paul, in a moment of authenticity, proclaimed, 'I am the chief of sinners,' yet he was beloved by God and used by Him mightily. Find comfort in the fact that, despite our failures, God still loves us and can use us for His glory!"

—Anthony Hendricks
Area Manager, Amazon Logistics

I Take Me Back

The room of terror,
restlessness and rage,
hunted me in the light of day.
A sunken mattress and a tattered quilt
housed tears that shook my windowsill.
I stacked cement blocks and boxes

against my door, yet night upon night
it came for more. I squeezed my eyes
'til sin was done, then wept until I peeked the Son

growing stronger as the years weaseled by
bankrupt tear ducts flooding dry
fear hunkering beneath buried shame
repossessing my dignity
once bound by invisible chains.

"She gave this name to the Lord who spoke to her: 'You are the God who sees me.'"

Genesis 16:13

"The pain of abuse is more than the pain from the action. There is also loneliness and shame because it seems no one sees or seems to care what is happening. All too often, the pain lingers into adulthood, develops into bitterness, and we repeat the process we hated. When evil seems to surround us, it is difficult to believe God is near. Hagar learned that God saw everything when people tried to harm her (Gen. 16). Naomi would also learn that God saw her and was planning good for her even when she did not realize it (Ruth 1:20-21; 4:14-17). No matter how frightening the room or life might seem, God is there and is working to ultimately bless our lives. Through God's grace and power, we can break the cycle of bitterness and become a blessing to others whose pain we know so well."

—Pastor Reggie Hundley

DADDY WAS MORE THAN HE WAS NOT

We dared not sit at the dinner table
before washing our hands. It was akin
to Pastor shouting when preaching
and no one in the congregation
saying, "amen."

> *Daddy was more than the stained oak floors*
> *on which I learned to navigate our home.*
> *He was the Douglas fir studs holding up the walls*
> *that caught me when I fell.*

Prayer preceded passing the chicken
or anointing the plate with a cornbread crumb.
See, Sunday dinner was communion and confession,
where my Daddy came from.

> *Daddy was more than his baby-back ribs on the*
> *charcoal grill*
> *that stuck to mine on the Fourth of July. He was the*
> *chest where my head*
> *could rest and safely store childhood pearls.*

Our Daddy taught us to stand tall, look you in the eye
when talking, and to open our mouth—
never mumble. He stood like the dogwood trees in bloom
lining our street in Georgia, yet his heart was humble.

> *Daddy was more than the cedar bunk beds*
> *we'd sink into at night. He was the bark that burned*
> *our deep convictions. So, when Daddy spoke, we listened.*

14 | *But GOD*

Sometimes his words were prickly
like fresh blue spruce needles, depositing
a sticky, woodsy aroma to my core—
like no one else's words could.

> *Daddy was more than my eyes and shoulders staring*
> *back at me, he was the full-bodied antique mirror*
> *reflecting*
> *the colorful liquor bottles and cigarette butts that I*
> *would leave hanging.*

Few knew that Daddy had no college degree.
He'd marinate in the Sunday paper—
from community to comics to obituaries
When he used a term we didn't know,
he'd point to the bookcase housing Bibles,
encyclopedias, and dictionaries—
without a word, we'd go.

> *Daddy was more than the world news,*
> *followed by "who, where, and what do you think?"*
> *He was our first teacher, steadily*
> *brewing us like his morning cup of coffee.*

He was more than his airborne profanity,
ignited by indignation. He was nylon thread
in a heavy-duty needle piercing, stitching,
binding, mending us like unfinished   leather.

> *Daddy was more than he was not—*

He prized a cruise to the Bahamas
a carafe of fine wine and steak (bone-in)
but was equally content with canned tamales,
a Budweiser and sleeping at the Economy Inn.

But GOD | 15

*Daddy was more than our family's black cast iron
skillet. He was a late-night game of checkers,
our audience when performing Jackson-Five hits,
Tom Jones's hips, and James Brown's splits.*

He was Red Foxx and Johnny Carson
blended at family gatherings. He taught
us that just like laughter—
love and justice have no color.

*Daddy was more than his ocean blue Lincoln Continental
in the driveway after work. He was the bathtub
filled with clean water, cloth, and Dial soap
that washed away our dead skin cells and dirt.*

Daddy once earned a standing ovation from Toastmasters,
then drove across town to shoot the breeze
with community hustlers,
    bent down
       on knees,
          rolling dice,
             playing craps under streetlights.

Daddy was more than he was not.

*He was more than the slate roof, shielding
from strong winds, fire, and pounding rains.
He was the winding roads with ledge drops and loose
boulders that led
me to a God Who sustains.*

My sleep was shaken more than once
by the voice of a man pleading with Dad
for a loan to salvage family and home.
Cash was passed like the tithe and offering basket,
then the shaking was gone.

*Daddy's feet stepped around God's house
more than they stepped in, but Daddy's days
were flooded with echoes of Amen.*

Daddy was more   than he was not.

"Honor your father and your mother, that your days may be long in the land that the LORD your God is giving you."

Exodus 20:12

"It is common for us to reach adulthood and reminisce on our childhood experiences and memories with our parents. As adults, we have two choices: we can be bitter and blame our parents for who they were not and what they did not do right, or we can choose to believe that they gave us the best they had to give and have gratitude for what they imparted, no matter how great or small. After all, we, too, will become parents, not perfect, but offering our best to our children."

—Jenae Tiki

HEALING FEATHERS

I awaken in West Nashville
to a place fresh as the patch over
the hole in my frontal lobe.
Fastened to my zero-gravity chair,
I escape hourly through the picture window
that parades a canopy of trees,
applauding the heavens.
Dancing silver maple leaves
parachute passed cardinals
and blue jays.
They feather-brush
the lush creek bed
with crimson and periwinkle.
Tiny warblers
dab pale yellow
onto my moment
of awe—when
a red-headed woodpecker
dashes onto the scene.
My eyes had never held a live
red-headed woodpecker.
Branch breaking at its landing,
long enough for wings to arrest its fall
and for me to inhale
the magnitude of its majesty—
Healing feathers.

But GOD | 19

"Then your light will break forth like the dawn, and your healing will quickly appear; then your righteousness[a] will go before you, and the glory of the Lord will be your rear guard."

Isaiah 58:8

"Healing begins in the spirit. Welcoming our healing God, Who created and cares for even the smallest of His creatures, opens our spirit to that healing."

—Kristie Beavers

MY NEXT BREATH

My nerves vacillate from shift change-vital checks
to serenity swaddled in skin-to-skin contact—

from the breast still flowing with milk and honey.
Liquid gold saturates your baby doll lips, throat, and tummy,

like a winter coat securing your survival beyond me.
My existence would cease fourteen years after yours began.

You had not savored hand-churned vanilla cream,
nor rode the wind's wings on a bike with outstretched arms,

nor navigated your first crush, first kiss, first love—
I have inhaled the atmosphere of Mount Denali,

showered in phalanges of the Florida Keys,
ate all the Tiramisu I craved in one sitting,

and painted my toenails teal and hot tangerine—on the same day.
I have humbled myself before Almighty God

Who created Palak Aloo and a mother who
stood in the gap when I was falling off the edge of the edge.

My son, you were my Joseph of Canaan, though my only child—
exiting my womb beneath the breast

that hastened me to the tomb's crest.
But I refused to go until I had no choice.

You were not an interpreter of dreams;
you were my dream.

But GOD | 21

When you crossed the threshold of my bedroom door,
rainbow-hues rode your shadow.

You were the collagen-elastin to my over medicated veins.
You gave light to my nights and length to my days.

I prepared for life while dying,
that you might come to know life while living.

I embrace the breath that became my last,
knowing you would take the next breath for me—
then another   and   another.

"And his mercy is for those who fear him from generation to generation."

Luke 1:50

My daughter was well love and loved well. Today, I can no longer give my daughter the gift of time, but I'm thankful for the time we gave one another when we could. Stop right now and schedule time with someone special in your life and do it again and again and again."

—Betty Lytle
Mother of Denise Lytle Trice and Mr. Bobby Lytle

INVASION

Rival
voices vomit acidic bile,
contaminating my perceptions
with droplets of delusions
on a rice paper reality.
Fused suns and moons bleed me of my sleep.
Voices swell like a Tanzanian pufferfish
as I shrink and grow weak—
unable to decipher
them from me.

The real transform
the imagined.
The imagined transforms
the real.

Something must change
because I can no longer feel
the entity I was
before the invasion.

I stare out the window of my shadows—

Impulsylvia sports an afro atop tattooed-on leggings
She spurts unsifted, unsolicited, unsavory truths
inconsequential to who's listening.
She presses "send" on unprocessed emails,
escapes politics by resignation and boldly embarks
upon uninvited, yet necessary conversations.

But GOD | 23

Then Magdela, who loves God more than a young goose with gravy.
I see her spread-eagled body over a spiked fence
where others beat dust from her like a rug
from a condemned house.
Then she pardons them; always pardoning
and loving, loving, and pardoning.
Adored, but her insides are pureed—

Quintessa is 5 foot 9, slender, poised,
with brow hairs perfectly postured.
Her air-brushed words edify any in her realm.
She incessantly whispers to me, "Wrap your wretchedness
in a garbage bag and trash it—
but not before tying a bow around it."

Intrepid, they are.

"Come to me, all you that are weary and are carrying heavy burdens and I will give you rest. Take my yoke upon you and learn from me; for I am gentle and humble in heart, and you will find rest for your souls. For my yoke is easy, and my burden is light."

Matthew 11:28-30

"Twenty-five years ago, my family founded The Center for Living and Learning for my brother who had been diagnosed with schizophrenia at the age of nineteen. Like many families searching for a place to get help for a loved one, we took my brother to several mental health facilities around the country, trying desperately to find care that would give him a respectable quality of life. In 1986, the family decided to purchase a farm in Franklin, Tennessee and start a residential program for my brother and others in need of a therapeutic, supportive, and caring environment in which to live. This facility gives people with severe and persistent mental illness hope for the future and the opportunity to function at their highest level possible. Mental illness is not contagious, but beginning to care, serve, and love those who are not like us can be."

—Fran Clippard

BIG MAMA'S DUMPLINGS

Big Mama had a large silver canister labeled "Love"
sitting on the shelf beside her seasonings.
She'd let me shake some in the pot
as the first and last ingredient
of everything we cooked,
especially her chicken and dumplings.
And if I forgot,
that container of love
would shimmy like Big Mama's shoulders
when she did the ragtime dance until I picked it up.
She had kneaded those dumplings
for decades—
the same slender, caramel fingers
that massaged cream into my eczema
and spanked me—only once.
Big Mama would wipe her fingers
on her cotton apron
while dropping dumplings
into blistering chicken broth.
The steam would burn her,
but she'd say,
"Child, your smile is worth more than a billion burns."
Then she'd dab flour onto my nose
and laugh.
She served me dumplings
in my favorite porcelain soup bowl
year after year until my brother broke it.
Seeing that broken bowl on the floor
reminded me of the chicken who was no longer
running around in the backyard and the holes in the ground
where the garlic and onion bulbs once rested comfortably.

Time has gone on an endless ride since Big Mama left us.
Today, as I gaze into my bowl of dumplings,
Big Mama's eyes stare back,
reassuring me like a glass of her homemade lemonade,
sipped on a scorching summer day.

As I inhaled the vapors rising
from her tender dumplings,
I could hear them whisper in Big Mama's
easy-going voice,
"It'll be ok, baby—"
The same words she uttered
when our mother died,
when her leg was amputated,
and when I became pregnant in college before marriage.
Wherever I am,
the aroma of thick slices of celery, chicken, and garlic cloves
blended and boiling blasts my senses
back to Big Mama's kitchen:
the porcelain rooster in the window
and the yellow Formica table, trimmed in aluminum.
I still feel Big Mama's velvety skin
as she grasps my hands, washing the flour and dumplings
from beneath my fingernails. She'd say, "Be still now, child"

I was always full when I left Big Mama's house.

"And he directed the people to sit down on the grass. Taking the five loaves and the two fish and looking up to heaven, he gave thanks and broke the loaves. Then he gave them to the disciples, and the disciples gave them to the people. [20] They all ate and were satisfied, and the disciples picked up twelve basketfuls of broken pieces that were left over."

Matthew 14:19-20

"Genuine love is likened to the pure love of Jesus Christ. Taking the most basic of ingredients and providing a meal that allows both the body and soul to be filled imparts not only lasting knowledge but allows the receiver to remember the lessons that this love provides. When one is within the presence of the Holy Spirit, the same love of a meal provided by a loved one's hands leaves the receiver full of love."

—Sunday Dell Perkins

Journey to Diagnosis

Entry #1

What's going on? First my keys, now my phone and purse. Who's moving my stuff? I put my keys on the nightstand beside our bedroom door. I left my purse on the kitchen table, and someone keeps moving it. Please stop moving my things! Misplacing or forgetting where I place things is just not me.

Entry #2

I confronted Caleb Sr. today about the cruel joke he's been playing on me by moving my things so I cannot find them. I made it clear how upsetting his behavior is, not to mention the time I spend looking for things. I know it's not like him to behave this way, but what other explanation could there be? Joshua, our dog, hasn't bothered my things since he was a puppy. Caleb Jr. stops by once or twice a week. It's just Caleb Sr. and I here most of the time. He was vividly livid as he yelled,

> *"You have been accusing me of moving and worst hiding your things for almost a year now. It stops today! I have never played practical jokes on you, and I have no reason to hide your belongings. Maybe you've forgotten, but I happen to love you."*

Caleb did not deserve the things I said to him, but nothing else makes sense to me.

But GOD | 29

Entry #3

My director requested I interview a potential employee today. A junior associate accompanied me to observe. I've conducted hundreds of interviews over the years and have never experienced what happened today. I can only describe it as "a blank moment." I looked at the woman for three minutes just trying to remember her name and why we were there. Finally, after much awkwardness, my junior associate said, "We are so happy that you are here today, Ms. _____." She promptly gave us her name. "Yes, Ms. Williams. And what led you to be interested in, let's see, which position? Yes, yes, that's correct. Well, why don't you tell us what you know about our company?" Fortunately, after her responses to my junior associate, it was as though a switch was turned on, and I remembered the interview questions, protocol, and purpose. I completed the interview with no trouble. Afterward, my junior associate asked if I was ok. I assured her that I was just exhausted and needed to get more sleep. Was I trying to convince her that I was okay or myself?

Entry #4

A month has passed, and I really thought things were getting better until today. I was sitting in my office at work this morning, and Caleb called to say he was awakened by the smoke detector and fumes from the kitchen. I had left eggs boiling and it started a small fire in the kitchen. He got to it before it was necessary to call the fire department, but what if he had not been home? I felt awful, but like Caleb said, it could have been worse.

Why am I engaging in these weird, dangerous behaviors that are so unlike me?

Entry #5

I did not get much sleep last night and arose early to prepare breakfast for Caleb Jr., who was visiting from college. After greeting me, he asked for gas money as usual. By then, I had started putting my purse in the same place so it was easier to find. He gave me my purse, and when I looked at the money, it was as though I was looking at something I had never seen before. It was another one of those "blank moments" when whoever or whatever had no meaning to me. After a few minutes of staring into my purse, I just shoved my purse into Caleb Jr.'s chest, and said, "There, get what you need." He looked at me as though I had lost my mind. I wanted to tell him that I might be—that is, losing my mind. I can only imagine his shock since he had kindly referred to me all his life as the "tightwad." Our eyes connect, knowing everything and knowing nothing of that moment as mother and son.

Entry #6

I took a week off, hoping stress was the culprit of these strange experiences. Unfortunately, not only have these experiences persisted, but Caleb Sr. seems more aware and concerned. We went grocery shopping yesterday. I put the groceries away in odd places and could not remember where I had put them. I would never put eggs in the laundry room or cereal in the linen closet, but I know that I had to have done it. Caleb went back to the store because he was convinced that we had left the bag with the eggs and cereal. Something very scary is knocking on my door, and I can no longer dismiss it as stress.

But GOD | 31

Entry #7

Yesterday, I had my most upsetting experience. I passed our subdivision driving home. I had done it several times lately, but I thought I was just distracted. Caleb had been teasing me about it, but yesterday was different. I got lost in our subdivision where we had lived for fifteen years. After driving around for twenty minutes, I parked in front of a house with a "For Sale" sign and wept. I had no other choice but to call Caleb. What is he going to think? I don't even know what to think. He asked me to describe what I saw, and he realized immediately that I was in our subdivision a couple of streets over. He guided me home through an ocean of tears and anxiety. When I got home, I could not look at Caleb. I dashed passed him and sprinted to the shower, then bed.

Embarrassment and fright were my inescapable companions last night.

Entry #8

This morning after Caleb left, I had to release, and I did. Here I am again, sobbing about this unknown entity that is destroying me and my relationship with my husband, son, and closest friends. I assumed it was me and the walls until Caleb Sr. pushed open our bedroom door and grabbed me. He held me for a half-hour before words were spoken. He knew. We both knew that something was wrong and that it was not getting better. I finally told him everything that I had been experiencing. Forgetfulness, getting lost coming home more frequently than he knew, little things at work, the money, everything. I felt so much better after telling Caleb. His response was exactly what I knew it would be, but I just didn't want to believe that something could be wrong with me. I am still hoping that I will wake up and be the way I was before all these things began happening. I know that sounds crazy after hoping the same thing for a year, but I do. We agreed that it was time to seek professional help to see what was going on with me. His presence and friendship have made each day bearable, but not easy.

32 | *But GOD*

Entry #9

Today is the day Caleb and I have looked forward to and feared. I was extremely nervous about what the doctor would think about me after telling him what I had been experiencing. When he walked into the room, my anxiety slowly softened like butter at room temperature as he gave me eye contact and directed questions to me although Caleb was present. I felt as though "he saw me and respected me." His kindness and nonverbal behavior made it easier to share. Caleb felt equally comfortable sharing his observations and concerns.

We inquired about possible causes of the blank moments. He said there could be several causes and it was a good idea not to speculate until we had gathered more information.

We asked if there were medications that I could take to stop these things from happening. He said that the first step was to identify the cause, then we would then be able to discuss treatment options. We asked if it could be a manifestation of chronic stress. He indicated that while chronic stress could aggravate as well as cause some of the symptoms, it was best not to speculate at this point. He scheduled me for a series of cognitive tests, interviews with neurologist, and brain imaging. We did not want to think the worst but were prepared for anything at this point.

I had more questions but more support and strength as I prepared to take up my cross.

Entry #10

We agreed not to tell Caleb Jr. anything until we had more answers. Halting my google searches was difficult, but each search made whatever was going on more of an undefeatable giant in my mind. I would wait for the results as my doctor had recommended. I pray the results come before tomorrow says goodnight.

Entry #11

The awaited answer arrived on the back of morning. The neurologist and my primary care physician gave me the desired but dreaded news. Today I found out that I have an early on-set form of Alzheimer's—a progressive brain disease. Caleb said they gave us all sorts of helpful information about current treatment options for Alzheimer's, but all I heard was that I have this progressive brain disease that has no cure.

I am still in shock because like many of my friends, I thought Alzheimer's was a disease for the elderly. I didn't know what to expect, but I did not expect this. I was even more surprised to find out that women are diagnosed with it more often than men, somewhat because we live longer. I have the Mild Alzheimer's Disorder, the stage at which most patients are diagnosed because the symptoms become more noticeable. They believe a gene mutation is the cause of my type of early-onset Alzheimer's, but health, environment, and lifestyle factors also contribute to the disease. I know, I feel like I have read everything ever published on Alzheimer's. Enough of that. We live to fight another day! Did you hear that, Diary? "We," not I, live to fight another day.

I don't have to hide it anymore.

Entry #12

The diagnosis has been hard for me to accept because it will greatly impact Caleb and our son. At least now, I know what I am fighting. I am taking steps to prepare to fight as best as I can and prepare my family to take care of themselves while they care for me as the disease progresses. I am working on improving my memory and delaying the progression of the disease if possible, and I'm reviewing the latest research on new Alzheimer's treatments. I will plan for anything that will help Caleb and Caleb Jr. to navigate life with me and Alzheimer's. I am now working two of my five days from home, so my benefits and pay have not changed. That has been a big relief! The support groups have been more helpful than I imagined they would be. Caleb and I really like this one couple who has been fighting the disease together for over a year now. Listening to what they are going through and have gone through gives us so much hope! Today, Diary, I am glad to be alive, even with this terrible disease. I am thankful that Caleb, our son, and close family and friends know what I am fighting moment by moment. I have found some solace in controlling what I can control.

"For I am convinced that neither death nor life, neither angels nor demons, neither the present nor the future, nor any powers, neither height nor depth, nor anything else in all creation, will be able to separate us from the love of God that is in Christ Jesus our Lord."

Romans 8:38-39

"I suppose there were numerous early symptoms of the condition. Signs that viewed collectively would more easily point one toward the direction of early onset dementia, or Alzheimer's, or whatever nasty pet word you secretly decided to call what is happening to your parent, your dad, your biggest cheerleader and historical co-conspirator for any silliness or adventure that you desired to embrace. But sitting in the neurologist's office and watching my dad attempting to scribble a written phrase at the doctor's request was painful until I was able to make out what he had written. 'I love my family' was written, barely legible. We embraced, cried, and continued to push on."

—Mrs. Ann Williams

NIGHT LIGHTS

Diamond dust sprinkled
against charcoal skies, dancing
with the moon's dim light,
lifting spools of darkness
from sunken souls
are nature's lanterns
illuminating
the night.

"If I say, 'Surely the darkness will hide me and the light become night around me, even the darkness will not be dark to you; the night will shine like the day, for darkness is as light to you.'"

Psalm 139:11-12

"Light, beauty, and strength can be found in the darkest of nights when we are looking for them."

—Irene Payne

BEREFT

Forty-four years of marriage gone—
your wing-tipped Bostonians still grace each room in our home.

Shivering as I close my eyes tonight.
in a house that shrieks when there is no light.

Sunrise seems much further away
the more I watch and wait for day.

Aches are my constant companions,
along with ceaseless television.

Meals are delivered during the week,
but your touch and laughter, I miss and need.

Walking, like taking a breath
requires I focus my every step.

Bathing bi-weekly is my main event—
in Epsom salt and oil of peppermint.

My greatest joys continue to be the simple things,
like melodies spring hatchlings bring

or observing a blooming lily,
chase loneliness from my face.

Crack of dawn ushers in my favorite time,
when morning's first silence mingles with mine.

Our scent on the pillowcase catches my tear,
carrying me through another moment.

But GOD | 37

"'He will wipe every tear from their eyes. There will be no more death' or mourning or crying or pain, for the old order of things has passed away."

Revelation 21:4

"God giveth and God taketh away"(Job 1:21). With every joyous bond of committed love, there will be loss. The feelings of bereftness, loneliness, lostness are deep and profound. Our faith can feel shaken. And yet, if we notice God's endless and fathomless gifts, the baby birds chirping, the deep petals of the mourning flower, even the gift of tears and memory, our love and gratitude will be steadfast. 'We are loved by an unending love,' Rabbi Rami Shapiro writes. Truly, this is God's blessing upon us all."

—Doris Ferleger

SHE REMEMBERS

The praises of her mockingbirds
broke silence of the night.
Brutal, bloody battles
awakened by new light.

Her rivers tasted the stale blood
of her sons and daughters—
the Mississippi, Cumberland,
and Tennessee waters.

Upon rocky peaks and valleys
of the Highland Rim,
her faith and tenacity
staunchly carried them.

Her cedars of Central Basin
stand permanently in salute
to fallen blades of grass
buried in their youth.

From rocky altitudes
of the Cumberland Plateau,
to flat and fertile
Gulf Coastal Plains,

her land preserves
with honor
their memories
and remains.

"Therefore, put on the full armor of God, so that when the day of evil comes, you may be able to stand your ground, and after you have done everything, to stand."

Ephesians 6:13

"No choice became a choice when I became a member of the United States Army. I had to give an account to a higher echelon. I was prepared mentally and physically for the challenges I might face as a soldier without input. Initially, I did not choose the military. I was drafted; nonetheless, I chose to do my best and strived to be the best at whatever I was directed to do while I served. I was totally devoted."

—Coleman March Sr.

- This poem first appeared in The Tennessee Magazine (online)

My Pecan Tree and Me

Brown-bold, tall, and tenacious
looking like any other pecan tree—
but it's not.
That pecan tree was sown by my grandaddy
the day Mama gave birth to me.
Whole pecans stir images of fists full of gold nuggets,
squeezed within my hands, reminding me that Grandaddy
gave that tree and me deep, wide roots to stand.

He couldn't have grasped that my
exigent existence
would emulate his breaking through rocky, resistant ground
to plant that tree—
poorly drained soil, stiff clay, his arthritic hands.
Grandaddy said nothing he'd ever planted had so struggled to take root
like that tree. It wrestled in its three-foot hole
like Jacob wrestled the Angel of the Lord at Penial—
dying before living our purpose was not likely for us.
Did Grandaddy know I'd grip the learned lesson of patience by waiting
winter after winter to eat pecans from that tree?

When it did bear fruit, my siblings and I never knew what Santa
was bringing,
but we eagerly awaited a brown box from Alabama filled with pecans.
When visiting in the summers, if I came home after the streetlights
lit, Grandaddy
would say, "Girl you can be as stubborn as that pecan tree of yours."
Then I'd say, "But you love it like you love me because
it gave you pecans in seven years instead of twelve."

But GOD | 41

My way and will shackled me like those pecans weighted down that tree.
Grandaddy would climb a ladder to shake those pecans loose at the right time.
A half century would pass before I would shake free—
resistant like those pecans I'd have to hammer-crack.
With jagged edges, the tiny brown pieces held core-cracking memories
of the time Grandaddy spanked me. It still stings, like pressure against thumb as I pushed shell back to reach meat.
Pecan debris often smacked me across the cheek.
Did Granddaddy and Big Momma expect my human years to yield the fruit
of that pecan tree? Did they envisage me gripping
God's hand like the roots of my pecan tree
clutched the earth when I quaked?

"That person is like a tree planted by streams of water, which yields its fruit in season and whose leaf does not wither whatever they do prospers."

Psalm1:3

"Wisdom is like a tree. At first, small and worthy of little note. But see the effect of time? How the roots grow stronger, deeper; how the limbs extend higher, seeking light. And look, after more time, how sweet the fruit."

—Bill Cochran

MOTHERS

I carried you through simmering summer months,
drudging up and down hills to get to class on time.
Your limbs quieted during lectures and discussion.

She   painted the nursery in your new home
and resigned her position at work—
so you'd hold her voice, scent, and touch in infancy.

I feel my body bursting with your body.
You squirm more, late into the evenings
when my day has   slowed   to   a   stew.

She had a baby reveal for you today.
Your room awaits you with diapers, crib, onesies—
all I want for you but can't give you.

I sampled smiles and kindness in your new home.
It was in the opened blinds, sweet aroma, and gentle hues,
inviting me to always be   your mother too.

"Many women do noble things, but you surpass them all"

Proverbs 31:29

But GOD | 43

"Adam called his wife 'Eve' because she was life-giving (Gen.3:20). When I think of a mother, I have come to think of motherhood as life-giving beyond physical life. A mother gives life to her household with her love, dedication, and a vision for her family. A mother's love binds her family. 'A wise woman builds her house and a foolish woman tears it down with her hand' (Pro. 14:1). A mother's role is awe inspiring because of the power she wields upon her household and generations to come."

—Donzaleigh Phillips
Guidance Counselor

A Life of Forgiveness

Considered saying, "I'm sorry,"
but my flesh screamed,
"For what?"
So we kept living
as though things were fine with us.

Finally asked your forgiveness,
hoping for genuine conversation.
Instead, you poured me a cup
of "everything is fine"
with a teaspoon of ostentation.

You infected hearts
with egocentric tales
dashed with partial truths.
So, tell me, why am I the one
apologizing to you?

You conveyed no remorse
for your sharply grated views,
conceivably distorted
by rage fuming ruthlessly.

Resistant to pleading my own case,
though at times my pores dripped war.
Revenge was consciously repressed
in hope of the relationship restored.

Burned holes through the mirror,
dissected my own heart,
instead of dancing on your flaws
and ripping you apart.

I remembered the times
God forgave me, for speaking impulsively.
His forgiveness did cost our Lord,
but it was freely given to me.

Bitterness could no longer nest here
cognizant of His mercy I continue to receive.
So I chose a life of seeking forgiveness
and forgiving repeatedly.

"Get rid of all bitterness, rage and anger, brawling and slander, along with every form of malice. [32] Be kind and compassionate to one another, forgiving each other, just as in Christ God forgave you."

Ephesians 4:31-32

"God forgives us for so much. How can we possibly withhold forgiveness from someone else? The hardest apology to accept is the one that was never extended. But one of the most liberating experiences is to forgive when there has been little or no remorse. The beauty is that God heals our hurtful scars, and brokenness when we submit to Him through forgiveness."

—Debbie Wheeler
Retired Educator

Her Reason to Live

I hear their voices
like his absence, ricocheting
off the popcorn ceiling, stroking the flat
ivory walls of our bedroom.
"Mommy will you make us
salmon croquettes for breakfast? Please Mommy!"
My face presses into stained oak floorboards,
cushioned by tears
dripping down two decades.

I raise my eyes to cuddle the gaze
of our twin daughters—
reflections of our love.
They blow oxygen into me
like their November birthday balloons,
pondering if I will inflate, deflate, or float away,
like their dad had that December—
promising to return to America.

I press my hands against the dented floor,
rising like my sticking windowsills.
I garner strength like seedlings
germinating in Styrofoam cups, needing water.
I feel a jolt as my girls
wait   and   stare
as though I were a blueberry muffin
being warmed in the microwave.

Planted now on bended knee,
core, spine, neck, I stretch for Sirius—
the star we'd search for from the patio
with their dad.

Like Canopus—
it was still within their reach.

But GOD | 47

"I have told you these things, so that in me you may have peace. In this world you will have trouble. But take heart! I have overcome the world."

John 16:33

"One should not reflect too long on lofty heights or dark depths. Most suicide notes contain the word 'hopeless.' Suicide is a permanent solution to what is usually a temporary problem. Even though life sometimes includes tough times, pain, heartbreak, suffering, and tears, it also includes joy, grace, peace, mercy, faith, and 'hope.' With God, all things are possible. We must cling to our hope in God's faithfulness as if our lives depend on it."

—Sharonese Henderson

HALF-TRUTH HALF-APOLOGY

I don't know what cunning words you crafted,
whether you tilted your head or perched your mouth?
Did deception drool, dance, or deluge
as you meticulously laid my ruin out?

I can hear your flattering tongue
uttering, "People just adore you."
Was it then you privately conjured
to publicly gut me through and through?

Your account was perfectly portrayed
with a fastidious portion of truth.
Then you impersonated a victim
in case credibility wasn't presumed.

Years later you invite me to a shaded corner
and extend a nebulous apology
whispered over water   with us   exclusively,
unlike your slanted narrative   that careened   the continent.

   "The Lord detests lying lips, but he delights in people
    who are trustworthy."

Proverbs 12:22

"We sometimes know we are wrong in a matter but have difficulty fully accepting it. Demonstrating healthy shame is fully owning up to our part in any relational conflict without justifying the wrong we've committed. Just as we should offer full repentance to God without excuses, we should confess and ask forgiveness of our neighbor with no excuses."

—Paul Martin Mulroy L.P.C. MHSP

PRIDE'S DEATH

I
It mimicked
empty shelves once holding
paper towels and tissue—
bare, alone, yet hungry to hear its name again, "Scott, Bounty, VIVA."
Pride wouldn't surrender like the faint footsteps
of shoppers and abandoned carts
in the emptied parking lot near closing time.
It was frozen like me—
in front of the fresh fowl section at Kroger,
clutching thigh and leg quarters in my right hand
and too few coins to purchase it in my left.
Theft was never a thought. Immodesty gradually melted
beneath howling stomach growls.
We were a pair of drifting gnats—
pupils sinking like suds flowing down the floor drain.
Any leftover pride went limp like loose skin on the
chicken quarters as I slung them back into the meat freezer.
It would be sardines and saltines with faucet water—
together again tonight   like us.

II
With no purse, plans, nor place to sleep the next night,
we crashed Church's Chicken—toothbrush, toothpaste,
soap, and rag in shrouded paper bag.
We divvied a two-piece snack (thigh and leg)
with biscuit and water, then rushed the sinks.
A tear drizzled to meet toothpaste at my lower lip.
Our reality was an undigested lump:
college graduates over forty. No home, no gas, half a cell phone,
and still not emptied of our pride.

The next morning would come like a slug on its tiptoes—

III

The foodbank was duck-tape
when food dwindled—
days, locations, and frequency limitations.
Early arrival and short lines were melted butter on hot brioche bread.
No personal information meant no peanut butter and pasta. Did Jesus and the disciples require indentification before feeding the hungry?
Speedy passage in and out preserved our dignity, unlike the pre-bagged food that dimmed it.
Plastic bags housed canned vegetables,
boxed crackers, and potatoes that eyed us like old associates
who feared contracting poverty.
We double-dutched with purple hearts who dared invite us to dinner—
it felt like Christmas.
Pantry's allowing us to select our own food
was like having our gas tank
filled for under three dollars a gallon in 2011.
The grocery bags now lay on our table—
not our Mayfair solid oak extendable table.
It was what we had. And God said, "It was good."

> "For I am persuaded that neither death nor life, nor angels nor principalities nor powers, nor things present nor things to come, nor height nor depth, nor any other created thing, shall be able to separate us from the love of God in Christ Jesus our Lord."
>
> Romans 8: 38-39

"Only on this side of Heaven can believers experience the life transforming joy and peace that Christ promises even as we are walking through the bleakest of conditions and circumstances. Forever sovereign and seeking only the best for His children, He orchestrates many an event on our behalf and allows us to witness His faithfulness while He performs one mountain moving miracle after another."

—Joshua Ellis

WOMAN OF SOFT STRENGTH

Woman of soft strength,
gentle peace,

your life is awe
inspiring!

Your eyes bring calm
to chaos,

your voice soothes
the angry heart,

bright intellectually,
yet humbly adorned.

Quiet   spirit
that moves mountains
monarchs cannot budge.

Words coated in mercy
that flow from Abba's love.

So candid, so kind,
Illuminating treasure in others.

You possess as a daughter
the hope of every mother.

Your laugh caresses hearts
as sandy shores the sea.

54 | *But GOD*

Woman of soft strength,
your life is awe inspiring.

Your giggle ignites spirits
that the world has turned cold,

Your energy radiates youth this life
could not grow old.

Woman of soft strength
and gentle peace,

cancer cannot erase
your living legacy!

"Your beauty should not come from outward adornment, such as braided hair and the wearing of gold jewelry and fine clothes. Instead, it should be that of your inner self, the unfading beauty of a gentle and quiet spirit, which is of great worth in God's sight."

I Peter 3:3-4

"The National Cancer Institute has released information indicating that 100,000 *new* cases of cancer are reported each year. This alarming data became significant to me recently as I was diagnosed with breast cancer for the second time in six years.

"Friends and loved ones ask many questions that pertain to how I cope with the pain and fear. The answer is simple. I am God's child. I will take responsibility for making good decisions to help heal my body. However, the wondrous news is that this struggle has reminded me of the comfort of my faith and dependence in God, the joy of receiving love from others, and the assurance that God's children are survivors in life and in death. I praise God for giving these gifts to all His children!"

In Him,
—Anita Anderson
Deceased Woman of Faith

This selection is dedicated to the memories of:

Thelma Givens
Carrie Sanders
Mildred Davis
Diane Walker DDS
Stephanie Renee Bell
Anita Anderson
Denise Lytle Trice
Lora Hall
Peggy Southerland
Virginia Sue Roberts

THAT DAY

Cold steel table, naked back,
IV in arm, dozing fast.
Compulsion to stop,
but it was too late for that.

Crushed heart, contorted hands
Too cowardice to comprehend
how my silence sanctioned
your embryonic life to end.

How would life have changed
had we allowed yours to be?
A second car seat and stroller for sure,
along with two toddlers to feed.

Childcare was the grizzly bear
since your dad and I worked full-time.
But God would have provided
if we had trusted Him and tried.

You couldn't utter your opinion—
Your dad and I were your voice.
Our tattered lives continued
though you were given   no choice.

I could not forgive myself for years
until I gave you a burial and names.
The pain will never subside,
but today, I remember you with love   not shame.

But GOD | 57

"…'Love your neighbor as yourself.'"

Matthew 22:39

"It was my senior year of high school, and all seemed well. I was dating the captain of the football team; I was a cheerleader and an honor student. We decided to take our relationship further because we believed that we were in love. We decided to be sexually active, and in no time at all, I was pregnant. Totally confused and afraid, I decided that I should have an abortion or try some other ridiculous method of getting out of my situation. With a lot of fear of what the future was going to hold for me, I chose to give birth to my child instead of having an abortion. She is a beautiful twenty-three-year-old young lady today whom I can't imagine life without her. Abortion appears to be the easy way out, but in the end, everyone involved loses. The child, the mother, the father and even the medical professionals who assisted must live with taking those precious lives."

—Mrs. Stephanie Fitzgerald

"The topic of abortion will always be an emotional debate. Whether you agree with abortion or not, studies show that the future effects on the mother's physical, emotional, spiritual, and mental health are negative. However, we must still love those who have made the decision to abort their developing child. It is only by showing the love of Christ that the cycle of abortion can truly be broken."

—Michael Scherer
Associate Pastor
Lakeshore Christian Church

It is Not

It is not darkness,
but light that refuses
to shine into that place.

It is not the argument
we had over breakfast this morning,
but years of bellowing silence.

It is not the gifts
you lavish upon me,
but the time you do not spend.

It is not the compassion you gave,
but the compassion
you withheld.

"For there is nothing covered that will not be revealed, nor hidden that will not be known."

Luke 12:2

"The less obvious are often culprits at the core of life's most egregious atrocities."

—Karen Nelson
Deceased Poet, Author, Retired Professor

(This poem first appeared in Fifty Word Stories on-line journal)

DEATH HURRIES ME

I stood like the weathered statues
as Dad was lowered into freshly broken ground.
The silence, white handkerchiefs, stares of finality—
clanged louder than my grief.

I drove from the cemetery,
viewing vines grip the mountain's waist
like Dad held my hand one summer evening
when a bug had flown into my ear.
The buzzing was tolerable,
but not the persistent pouncing on my ear drum.
The louder I screamed the tighter Dad's grasp grew.
Death hurries me to hold someone's hand like that.

Upon entering Dad's apartment, I was embraced by Aramis—
his leather Chypre cologne.
When I long for his voice or crave his smile,
I take a deep whiff of Aramis.
Death hurries me to remember.

In the kitchen, the faucet drips—
Dad had scheduled for repair.
The droplets intrude upon my sadness.
I turn off the water.
Death hurries me to drink more before the stillness.

The stainless-steel stove was still wearing crumbs
from fried crappie.
Dad often asked for liver and onions with gravy,
pot roast, mashed potatoes, turnip greens, and macaroni and cheese.
Death hurries me to serve others while I can.

I took the twelve stairsteps to Dad's bedroom. Gently leaning
my head against his on the morning of his death, Dad shared a
deep longing
to have learned to listen and obey God earlier.
Death hurries me to be sensitive to the voice of God.

He poured out regrets—his last week of life—like opened
cans of beer
we'd empty together when we visited his father.
Death hurries me to see my flaws clearer than those of others.

My children and I had sung, "My Girl" by the Temptations
to him weeks
before at the foot of his bed. He laughed so long, so loud until he
could not.
Death hurries me to laugh with others.

My youngest brother and I sat on the steps outside Dad's apartment.
Everyone was gone—
We had removed every chair, pot, and suit. We wept.
Death hurries me to taste life's most fragile moments.

> "Teach us to number our days, that we may gain a heart of wisdom."
>
> Psalm 90:12

> "Life is uncertain, and Death is sure. We are all equal only in the sight of God and in the days He grants us on this earth. How we use our time and talents will depend on where we will spend eternity. Decisions and not conditions are what control our lives!"
>
> —Lucille Allen,
90 years young

DISTRACTIONS

slip in like line-cutters in rush-hour traffic—
embezzling your energy, time, attention, and mind.
It is the broccoli floret that hi-jacked your fork
on your deep dive for the couscous,
the mosquito that bites your leg
while you are shooing the fly from your head.
It is that thing, that thang, that beep, that bang
that causes you to lose your place, nick your face
when shaving your beard or arching your brow.
Distractions have driven me away
from Present's place
to something, anything, of less significance—
like the time I went bike riding instead of listening
to my aunts and uncles share stories from their childhood.
Or the times I stayed up late on a Saturday night,
then couldn't make church on Sunday.

Distractions will consume your life, balloon in your life, unless you catch them before they discover you are ever absent.

> "Finally, brothers, whatever is true, whatever is noble, whatever is right, whatever is pure, whatever is lovely, whatever is admirable-if anything is excellent or praiseworthy-think about such things."
>
> Philippians 4:8

"I had determined to sit down with my Bible and spend time with my Lord, but that plant needs some water, and oh, I think the coffee is ready, and is it going to rain today? The din in my head is like a clanging cymbal, distracting me, but God has taught me to say 'yes' to the important and weed out the less important."

—Melanie Baker
Women's Ministries Director
Lakeshore Christian Church

LITTLE WORLD CHANGED FOREVER

I study our framed family of four.
Daddy's German leather jacket
no longer drapes the corner tree
in the foyer beside our front door.

My wobbly knees
begin to crumble, clash, and clang
like fenders the day of the accident—
when me and Mommy's lives
were forever changed.

I still see Daddy in the kitchen
frying chicken and steaming crawfish boil
in our jumbo stainless-steel pot.
Wonder if he still remembers
us or if death made him forget.

"Look Mom, there's Sissy too—
crawling, scrambling around
the dining room table and chairs."
Her stare is bidding me to chase her,
but I know   Sissy isn't there.

We'll never peek out the window
shoulder to waist again—
to see who's ringing the glockenspiel
or galloping through our cornflower field.

But Daddy and Sissy's heartbeats
pump through the picture above the buffet.
Their ebony eyes catch me
on days when I've fallen into fate.

64 | *But GOD*

Their hands still clap, offering me high-fives
and pulling me in like the crawfish boil.

"He will swallow up death forever, and the Lord God will wipe away tears from all faces…"

Isaiah 25:8

"A child's response to the death of a loved one, while different from that of adults, can also be overwhelming. Young minds do not fully comprehend why their loved ones are no longer with them, but where human understanding ends, our Lord and Savior Jesus Christ intervenes to rid our hearts of void. As we nestle in His arms, He embraces us with the everlasting love, comfort, strength, and peace that only He can provide."

—Lesa Williams
Former wife of deceased First Sargeant Lesly Williams, and mother of deceased daughter Alana Williams.

GROWTH

Who I was yesterday
is not who I am today.

Who I am today
is not who I will be tomorrow.

Who I will be tomorrow
is not who I will be in eternity.

"So, neither the one who plants nor the one who waters is anything, but only God, who makes things grow."

I Corinthians 3:7

"Change is inevitable, yet we cling desperately to the past. For those we love, we resist change because it upsets our own world, or we try to force the loved one to change into the mold we envision for them. This leads to conflict and stifles growth. God usually surprises us with the changes He brings into our lives, but it brings true growth. Are you ready to be surprised?"

—Loretta Gjeltema

SMILE AGAIN

Summon laughter
from childhood days
of chasing butterflies
through fields of hay.

Lightening bugs making magic
on the edge of dusk.
Older boys spraying youngsters
with their outdoor musk.

Bumblebees bounce
from blossom to bloom,
and sunrays dancing
hopscotch in my room.

Cool creek bed water
twice tickle my toes
'til Grandma's baked cookies
charm my nose.

I sink into softness
of my cashmere throw
Mom swaddled me in
through winter's cold.

Come, let sweet honeysuckle
awaken our tongues
to times where happier
days once hung.

"I lift up my eyes to the hills where does my help come from? My help comes from the Lord the maker of heaven and earth."

Psalms 121: 1-2

"When you're going through one of life's storms and everything around you seems to be in despair, it's hard to remember from where we draw our strength. With God's grace, we are reminded to move on from a season of loss and despair back to joyful life where pain is now a memory, bittersweet and wrapped in peace."

—Andrea Robinson

SOULMATE

He hears my intimate thoughts before   I speak.
He hums the song in my heart before   I sing.

He escorts me to breakfasts with dawn
and evening dinners roasted by fire

His voice soothes.
His touch rules.

My soulmate

grasps my hands, and our fingers begin a familiar dance
choreographed with intricacies   not fashioned by chance.

Whispers of "I love you, I love us" is often heard
when he senses my need for an encouraging word.

His arms hold.
His Godly wisdom enfolds.

My soulmate

washes me in the word as I sleep,
Praying prayers of protection over me.

His presence ushers peace to my restless soul.
He bathes me in his love as mine unfolds.

He alone senses when I am present but gone
and says, "Where are you?"

He is my soulmate.

But GOD | 69

"That is why a man leaves his father and mother and is united to his wife, and they become one flesh."

Genesis 2:24

"Marriages are not meant to be perfect; only the person to whom you are married is meant to be the perfect one. So many of us decide to marry a person in less time and with less consideration than we take in purchasing our first vehicle, something that is far less important in the long run. Fifty-two years, two daughters, and three grandchildren later, I strongly encourage you to pray, watch, and wait until God sends you your Soul Mate."

—Mrs. Liz Warren
Retired Principal
Virginia Beach, VA

SNAPSHOTS FROM CHILDHOOD

Smudged faces, dangling laces,
toys scattered throughout the den.
Chitter chatter crowned with laughter
and flashes of snaggletooth grins.

Snuggling with Disney movies
for the millionth trillionth time,
munching on popcorn and smoothies
with a burst of clementine.

Bowling birthday parties,
Christmas concerts at school,
endless soccer games
before pouncing in the pool.

Hot, muggy road trips to relatives,
with loads of preferred snacks and picnic stops.
We'd hum family favorite songs
To hush duets by Dad and Mom

Did I cherish those moments
that rapidly dissipated
like the only real snowman
we built   with Dad?

But GOD | 71

"By wisdom a house is built, and through understanding it is established; Through knowledge its rooms are filled with rare and beautiful treasures."

Proverbs 24:3-4

"Images of family in their daily routine reveal humor, affection, and shared values—while traditions that help to celebrate special days create a colorful perception that we delight in being family. 'We belong, and we are cherished.' These moments are fleeting, and the wisdom is in the directive to 'cherish the moments,' to choose to treasure relationships. So, I make a choice. I choose to praise God, to celebrate my grandchildren, to encourage my children, and to kiss my husband. I choose to capture every moment in my heart and to live without regret."

—Sherri Rogers
Masterpiece Ministries

Missing You

Longing to hear your voices,
awaiting your texts or calls.
Gone are clanging pots and pans
and fingerprints on the walls.

No dirty dishes in the sink,
no trampled t-shirts on the floor.
The silence we once coveted
now lingers behind your door.

No "Pick me up," nor "Drop me off,"
nor "I'll be late getting home from school."
Suddenly, it comes to a halt,
and we're left pondering what to do.

No "Clean your room before you go out,"
nor "Turn that deafening music down!"
Just sweet moments reminiscing
of joyful times when you were still around.

"Start children off on the way they should go, and even when they are old they will not turn from it."

Proverbs 22:6

"As a young mother, I remember thinking my children would never grow up. Many times, they would squeal with delight as they escaped from an imaginary monster or surprised their father by hiding behind the door. I can still feel the warmth of little hands on my face as they demanded my total attention. Birthdays, holidays, and family gatherings are all etched in memory. 'Missing You' reminds me of the precious times with our children that were priceless."

—Theresa Chaplin
Teacher

True Love

seeks you out in the morning like the sun settles on the mountain's peak.
It cools and soothes your tired body beside the river's bank.

It is the sway of a wooden bench-swing affixed to the giant oak,
where our small talk grew legs and danced into the dawn

True love is the evening breeze resting upon your brow
and taking your pulse at the finish of a frantic day.

It is the quiet between us as tree frogs present their nightly orchestra
while we nestle beneath blankets under the half-moon's aura.

You are my safe place to run, like a field mouse dashing
to its home in the crawl space, secure from the fennec fox.

It is that breath you take in   and let out   after parking in your
driveway following a distant, draining road trip.

True love magnifies life's sunsets and lessens the hornet stings.

"My beloved is mine and I am his; he browses among the lilies."

Song of Solomon 2:16

"When the foundation of your love is God and you trust Him, everything else will be fine."

—Mrs. Robin Mardis
Wife and Mother of Five

First Vacation

Our striped matching luggage
lounged in the car for weeks,

witnessing our anticipation,
bursting like canned drinks left in the freezer.

The destination moment arrived
like that awaited meal after a fast.

Our cottage greeted
us with waving palms—

you expected undisturbed rest
while I was fueled for adventure.

You wanted to sleep well beyond dawn's arrival
while I wanted early morning walks with the sea.

You declined housekeeping service
while I wanted it twice a day.

You expected it to be solely us
while I hoped to converse with the natives.

Today our richest excursions
are inimitable moments that cost nothing.

"Take me away with you—let us hurry! Let the king bring me into his chambers."

Song of Songs 1:4

"There is no greater gift you can give to one another than replenishing yourselves and renewing your love and commitment to your marriage. There is no substitute for quality time spent together, becoming more intimate with God and with each other."

—Darrell and Annie Heaton

Mornings

Sparrows whistling and singing,
alarm clocks rocking and ringing.
Coffee creeping up the stairs,
knock, knock, I hear Grandma's prayers.
Sis commandeering the bathroom in rollers,
Mom fast walking the twins in their stroller.
Shepherds barking, people jogging,
cars bumper to bumper,
T r a f f i c   s t o p p i n g.
Commuters flashing lights and blowing horns,
farmers plowing fields and harvesting corn.
Cargo trains raging and rumbling,
children chasing buses and stumbling.

Dad checking the weather and news,
lost his car keys, just found his shoes.
Oops, bumblebee flew into the windowpane.
Late for check-in, can't miss my morning plane.
Bullfrogs gawking,
roosters squawking.
The goldfinch and cardinal sprinkle their hues
against this frantic morning's new day dew.

> "If I rise on the wings of the dawn, if I settle on the far side of the sea, even there your hand will guide me, your right hand will hold me fast."
>
> Psalm 139:9-10

"Mornings are a beautiful part of the day. With the onset of dawn coupled with light dew in the grass, it signals the beginning of a twenty-four-hour day that we are given. For some, it's the start of a hectic day at work, while for others, it may be the beginning of organizing our home for a full day with our young children or other responsibilities. Another morning is another opportunity to live life to the fullest, share our God given talents, and make a difference in a world that really has a lot to offer... if we can only see it in the morning.

Whatever your endeavor may be, understand that most of all, it is a blessing."

—Rhea Kinnard

FREEDOM

woke with me this morning.
The color and fit of his suit
and tie no longer competed
with my cup of dandelion tea.
The kitchen clock accounts for his return,
but my eyes no longer attach to it like a chef to his timer.
No more examining collars for foreign hairs or foundation smudges.
My breath catches a fresh scent—
could that be Freedom?
Compulsions to sniff like a baying bloodhound,
empty pockets, and scrutinize phone logs
have vanished—
it is you, Freedom. Punier than imagined
for such a robust
reality.

Gone is the duress to call him two dozen times during the day.
Gone is the need to remind him of our twenty years.
Gone is the need to account for every coin he spends.
Gone is tracking car, bike, and foot mileage.

Morning kisses my cheek
as Freedom saturates every suspicion.
I pray passed him in the night—
and each that followed,
instead of sleepwalking to peruse his briefcase.
It   all   dropped dead beside my captivity
moments before her tears meet my ears.
I hang up the phone this time

and take our children to the beach.

"It is for freedom that Christ has set us free. Stand firm, then, and do not let yourselves be burdened again by a yoke of slavery."

Galatians 5:1

"No marriage is perfect, and each requires work, patience, forgiveness, and understanding. The covenant of marriage was intended to be one where spouses are loved, loyal, and protected. When it fails to be that, we must remember we are still loved, complete, and never alone."

—Joyce Colden
Retired School Psychologist

Thought You Would Come to Me

Misrepresented,
misunderstood,
You could have come to me.
I trusted you would.
Instead, you took the lies and ran,
like beads of water hopscotching
in a hot, greased frying pan.
Scattering, then fading away.
Too angry to listen
to what I had to say.
Easier to accept the lie
than to look yourself in the eye.

Thought you would come to me,
but you didn't.
Why?

"Everyone should be quick to listen, slow to speak, and slow to become angry, for man's anger does not bring about the righteous life that God desires."

James 1:19

"Some of our greatest disappointments as believers are connected to the shortcomings of other believers. We expect our siblings in Christ to seek out veracity, as opposed to blindly accepting a lie. We can be grateful, however, for the wise instruction our Father provided for even these situations. We are commanded to love, even when we are misperceived or misrepresented."

—Tia Mitchell

JUST BECAUSE

I dipped you a chilled cup of agua
to drench your shriveled lips—
dry, cracked skin assaulted
by the afternoon sun
and rising desert winds.

Just because...

I cooked your favorite meal
of Egusi soup with cocoyam fufu.
Then watched your smile blossom
from Lagos to Cameroon,
like the vibrant hibiscus in the kitchen window,
kissed by the half moon.

Just because...

Scooped you up in my red pick-up
for a Sunday evening drive
down winding Tennessee back roads,
passed Angus, deer, American toads
framed by cattails and Queen Anne's lace.
There—painted, perfect contentment on your face.

Just because...

But GOD | 85

"The goal of this command is love, which comes from a pure heart and a good conscience and a sincere faith."

I Timothy 1:5

"True happiness and contentment grows within us when we are intentional to show pure love and kindness to others. How easy to freely give a smile, touch a hand, or listen with a quiet, open heart? Be a shining light to someone's darkness with a simple, heartfelt gift of yourself!"

—Cindy Gossett

Break me, Mold me, Make me Yours

You thought your whipping words
would leave me liver-limp,
powerless to stand?

A broken, bitter woman—
never to rise again?

You overestimated your aptitudes,
Like crawling toddlers who imagine they can walk
Then crumble—crumble like a wilting celery stalk.

Break me, mold me, make me Yours.

You thought that losing my Hudson Hornet
would bring me to disgrace? Instead, it sifted me like wheat,
fortifying my love for God, mankind, and faith.

You thought masked bruises over fractured bones
would crush my spirit like a crumpet through and through?
My bruises healed, but can you live
with the demons possessing you?

Break me, mold me, make me Yours.

You thought tragic deaths
of my confidants would surely seal my coffin?
You leered as I buried them   like human buzzards balking.
You thought lynching me professionally
and living in cheap hotels
would breed bowels of despair
my dark skin could not repel.

Break me, mold me, make me Yours.

You thought slander and false accusations
would make me tuck, turn, and run,
like cockroaches scattering
through crevices from the sun.

You thought the pressures of an absent father
would compress me like a crepe,
but hope inside refused to die,
so I love instead of hate.

You thought fear would take me hostage,
assassinate my dreams,
but the Spirit of the living God
has resurrected me.

"Consider it pure joy, my brothers and sisters,[a] whenever you face trials of many kinds, because you know that the testing of your faith produces perseverance. Let perseverance finish its work so that you may be mature and complete, not lacking anything."

James 1:2-4

"During the battles, the burdens, and the valley experiences, I am overwhelmed with the oppression. I find myself asking, 'Why Lord?' Earnestly praying, even pleading, that You will immediately rescue and relieve me from the pain.

"When I come through, I reflect and realize there was purpose in the test. It is clear that because of it, not despite it, I am stronger, wiser, and more mature in the profession of my faith. You did not abandon me nor forsake me. You were there, guiding me and carrying me through the storm."

—Brenda Neumon Lewis

You Are Not My Enemy

Riding my pulse,
like a reef-break wave
with subliminal tension
beneath a water grave—
are our recurring disputes.
"Why not tell me
our cell phones
were scheduled to be turned off?"
Because it's my responsibility
to keep them on.
"And why didn't you tell me
the rent was past due?"
Because paying our rent
is on me, not you—
his words zoomed
passed me with the wooden barstool.
When it's over, you say,
I meant no harm,
but it is done.
When your logic hemorrhages,
asphyxiating calm,
we become incensed,
waterboarding our love—
serenity clawing for solid footing
that's barely afloat.
Raised   breastbone,
squeezed   pounding fists,
and   bulging   eyes—

You   Can   Stop   This
habitual loss of control
that we intermittently
allow to unfold
against us.

"Better a patient person than a warrior, one with self-control than one who takes a city."

Proverbs 16:32

"The hardest thing to do, in this earthly life, is to remember that God has commanded us to use self-control in all situations. A tender smile or gentle touch cools the fires of wrath. Swallowing anger is the epitome of humility."

—Nells Wasilewski,
Poet/Author/Speaker

SEE ME

WE NEVER TOLD ANYONE

Sat down to a loaded breakfast
of fatty bacon on blackened toast.
Dad guzzled orange juice on the rocks,
chased by rum and coke.

I sprinted for the newspaper
before he could even ask,
but his screaming still commenced
about all my undone tasks.

Mom sat like a weighted figurine
mounted on a thin wafer—
too disconcerted to speak,
knowing glances were safer.

Years of Dr. Jekyll and Mr. Hyde
yielded tension more toxic than London's smog.
Family dynamics we labored to disguise
sunk Momma's heart like a frozen log.

Pot roast too pink, fried okra is too crisp.
Time to grab packed suitcases, keys, and split
before a broken bone or bruised wrist
sends someone to the emergency room.

Profanity pierced the solid oak doors
and shook all the gypsum board walls
while searching for bottles in cabinets
preceded Dad's grumbling and falls.

But GOD | 95

We never told anyone

Pleas for forgiveness the next morning
were as certain as Mom giving him "one last chance."
Then the cycle to keep our secret
would launch   all   over   again.

"For whatever is hidden is meant to be disclosed, and whatever is concealed is meant to be brought out into the open."

Mark 4:22

"We often think that our silence protects the family when in fact, silence adds to the hurt, burden, and pain that the children carry—sometimes forever. Only with God and other interventions will the alcoholic, and those who are a part of the disease cycle, be able to break free to live a life of emotional, mental, and spiritual stability. For many, this never occurs, so the family secret perpetuates itself generation after generation. Talking with a trustworthy adult, such as your pastor, counselor, or teacher, can be the beginning of a healthier you and ultimately, a healthier family."

—JB Kearney

SEE ME!

Passed you in my wheelchair.
Like many, you stared
but did not speak.

Held your glance in mid-air,
hoping you'd maneuver
beyond my burns
to see Me there.

I heard you ask yourself,
"I wonder what happened
or if it was congenital?"
It would have been ok
for you to ask me.

Wish you would have   paused
to simply

say "hello"

to a person
who is more
than their   disability—

a dreamer
who has whimsical thoughts (at times),
just like you,

a dancer stirred
by the rhythm of Djembe drums,
to hop up and break out in hip rolls
if I could   too,

But GOD | 97

a friend who likes
when you share your heart
over a grilled cheese at lunch,

a cheerleader
who will support you
against the world,
though based on a hunch,

a person who yearns
for you to see Me
beyond my scars
and disability!

> "The king asked, 'Is there no one still alive from the house of Saul to whom I can show God's kindness?' Ziba answered the king, 'There is still a son of Jonathan; he is lame in both feet.'"
>
> II Samuel 9:3

> "There are many people with disabilities all around us, and I happen to be one. I love music, basketball, volunteering, writing, and spending time with friends. I'm outgoing, independent, responsible, and fun-loving. Really, I'm not that different from everyone else. My disability doesn't define me. Although people don't always see past my disability or understand how it can actually be a positive force in my life, I live life to the fullest every day, knowing that one day, people will finally 'see.'"
>
> —Amy Saffell, 28
Miss Wheelchair Tennessee 2007

If Acorns Were Cash

they too would desire to be your king.
They'd expect you to hoard them like squirrels,
burying them beneath your mattress spring

Would you use your acorns
to purchase shoes when your rent is due?
Would you find yourself bowing
to acorns that once bowed to you?

They'd encourage you to only befriend
those with a million acorns in store
and to believe you could never be happy
unless you amassed a million more.

If acorns were cash,
you might squabble and contest
after a loved one transitions,
leaving an ambiguous bequest.

If acorns were cash,
you'd ruminate about them
all   day   long.   Acorns
might become your excuse
for doing others wrong.

Would you spend more time accumulating acorns
than being with   family,
who your finest acorns could not replace,
even if you owned every acorn tree?

But GOD | 99

"'All this I will give you,' he said, 'if you will bow down and worship me.' Jesus said to him, 'Away from me, Satan! For it is written: Worship the Lord your God and serve him only.'"

Matthew 4:9-10

"Money and credit may be the foundation of our economy; however, it is a mistake to make it the foundation upon which we live our lives. What we do with our money is a great indicator of what is important to us. Does money control you, or do you control your money?"

—Wade E. Miller II

Comparti Alegria

Yesterday I captured white clouds
that swept softness across the skies.
Today they transformed into cotton sleds,
beckoning me to ride.
Tomorrow the clouds will sail away,
beyond firmaments unknown.
I bundle them in wooden baskets
to share as I journey home.

"Your love has given me great joy and encouragement, because you, brother, have refreshed the hearts of the Lord's people."

Philemon 1:7

"If there is nothing else we take from life, nothing else we learn, it should be to love others the way God intended us to. We should take whatever happiness we receive, double it, and put it right back into the world. You will always find purpose in loving others."

—McKayla Anne Rockwell
Editor

HOLD ON!

Middle school is like
riding a new bike
over jagged speed bumps.

Better squeeze those handles
octopus-tight
to survive this ever evolving
time of life!

Maneuvering homework
and relationship boulders,
walking while texting
with backpack over shoulder.

A bus load of concerns
about what everybody thinks—
how I dress, am I cool
enough to invite to the skating rink?

Obsessed with weight, height, and hair
Fretting tests and giving speeches
on places you'll never go
while daydreaming of beaches.

Emotions and blemishes out of control,
a changing physique you wait to unfold,
but before you give up or give in—
hold onto the words of a friend!

Remember that time
you left your lunch at home,
and you were so concerned
you'd have nothing to eat,
then lunchtime came around,
and six friends shared their meals?

102 | *But GOD*

Remember when your mom
was late picking you up several times one week,
and instead of your teacher becoming annoyed,
she bid you to erase the board and gave you a special treat.

What about when you won "Student of the Month"
for being courageous on the playground
by discouraging a fight?

Hold on to people and principles
that really matter most.
Pop wheelies on the positives,
brake on negative notes!

Hold on to the hugs and kisses,
playing ball or tag at the park.
Hold on to exceptional memories
that inspire and tickle your heart.

Hold on to beloved hobbies,
favorite books, and songs.
Hold on to those who celebrate,
challenge, and cheer you on!

Hold on to laughter
and the truth
that you are beautiful,
whether others think so or not!

Hold on to the hope
of a tomorrow
better than the day
you just got!

Hold on to
high expectations
to be honest,
prepared, and true.

Hold on to
those rare, core jewels
that make you
undeniably you!

Dedicated to Middle School students at Lead Southeast and Intrepid College Prep in Nashville, TN and all over the world!

"Jesus Christ is the same yesterday, today, and forever."

Hebrews 13:8

"Middle school is undeniably a season of change, a time when we discover who we are and more about what we believe. Those mindsets are fragile and still require the nurturing and support of the community around them. At times, students may appear misguided or lacking conviction, but ultimately, we have to remember they are still kids, and they necessitate the type of unwavering support only a healthy, mature adult can champion."

—Chris Elliott
Middle School Principal

Respect for the Blue

Synchronized ripples
waltz upon the lake,
curving, then twirling
to caress grassy banks.
Suave surface calmness
reflecting the gaze
of those mesmerized
by her dancing waves.
Stroking her silky
sapphire body
while riding her bends
in cedar canoes,
oblivious of perils
befalling those who
show no respect
for dangers of the Blue.

"The earth is the LORD's, and all its fullness, the world and those who dwell therein. For He has founded it upon the seas, and established it upon the waters."

Psalm 24:1-2

"Water is ever-changing. It fits only the space it is given. Water is like humans' ever-changing nature over the course of time. Humans have their barriers just like water does. Water is beautiful, gives us life, and we can't live without it. Water is also destructive, powerful, and its big waves can bring down cities."

—Lesly Jamal Williams
David Lipscomb University student

"I Got Game"

Trained tenaciously
mastering the game.
Sacrificed my temple,
endured aches and strains.

My team became like family.
When in the zone,
them and the basket are all I see.

I live for the fans' cheers
and adrenaline rushes.
When it's game night,
I'm* Duke for my Duchess.

Slam dunk, basketball goal.
No time to study.
Just eat, practice, and roll.

Time came to graduate.
Duchess is accepted to college.
I waited for scholarships,
hoping I could follow.

Scouts said, "Your game is tight,
but we can't admit you to our school
cause your grades aren't right."

Years passed working at a local store,
friends returning home on Spring Break
rarely hit me up anymore.

How could I think it was just about the Game?
Two years after high school,
few folks in town even remembered my name (including Duchess).

But GOD | 107

"Physical training is good, but training for godliness is much better, promising benefits in this life and in the life to come."

1 Timothy 4:8

"Many young athletes fall victim to focusing solely on sports. They neglect to devote similar energy and effort to their schoolwork and developing other dimensions of their person and character. Success in sports is great for some who are uniquely gifted and have worked hard to improve their skills, but that does not guarantee a future as a professional athlete. However, being a well-rounded person who has learned the discipline required to be a good student and citizen prepares them for success in life. We must encourage young athletes to see the big picture."

—David Matikke Jr. M.A.
Highschool Teacher and Soccer Coach

Dad Told Us

The five of us were stacked
like books upon his lap.
He strained for the perfect words,
but all he did was wept.

With sullen, sunken shoulders,
 drooping jaws and wilted head,
 Dad muffled through tear-filled mucus.
"Momma, your Momma is dead!"

His body went limp
 as we tumbled to the wooden floor.
 Violent shivers and screams of
"We want our mommy now!"

The hours that followed
were numb, still, and cold,
like our mother's hands
we would never hold… again

"Blessed are those who mourn, for they shall be comforted."

Matthew 5:4

"In the tenderness of our mourning, we often, in our grief, seek the living amongst the dead. But for those in Christ, there is no death. Though our grief is real, loss tangible, God becomes the covering for our... father, mother, husband, wife... lost loved one. Strengthened, tested, and proved, how we walk through our difficulties becomes our greatest testimony."

—Cecilia Warren
Mother of two

CHILDHOOD FEAR

was that force I felt as an infant screaming
while staring at the ceiling fan.
My lips latch my mother's nipple; I taste relief.
After birthing my youngest brother,
Momma stopped smiling.
Daddy came home   later and   later.
One fall morning, an older cousin found Momma
in fetal position moaning, "Call
                             for
                        help."
The flashing red siren of the ambulance, coalesced with adult despair,
shook the floor of my existence as it sped away with Momma.
Sleepless nights met me before age five.
Images of our next-door neighbor who had burned in a fire
zoomed in and out beside Momma's motionless body.
She never came back after the fireman put her in the ambulance.
I knew Momma was not coming home again—
Death wailed at Momma's funeral.
My tears would not run and play that day.
It felt like my hair was not greased and braided for weeks (though it was),
and there were no grape, frozen Kool-aide cups for dessert.
After the funeral, as I lingered behind the kitchen door,
my grandparents pleaded with my father to separate
my five siblings. They said it would be easier on him—
the screen door double-slapped the frame as my father thundered
out with the five of us.
Mental somersaults dominated like the smell of mothballs

But GOD | 111

Momma would put in the closet corners:
    Who will make us cream of wheat,
        give us bubble baths,
            sew, wash, and iron our clothes,
                make my little brother stop crying—
                    teach me to be a woman?

"See that you do not despise one of these little ones. For I tell you that their angels in heaven always see the face of my Father in heaven."

Matthew 18:10

"You never know what others have gone through in life. The events and experiences that have shaped them, the frightening or painful memories they carry. "May I remember that as I go through my day, and may it give me a spirit of compassion and understanding as I interact with the world. Lord, use me to perform acts of kindness or to offer a word of comfort and encouragement to those in need."

—Mrs. Renee Hicks
Retired School Psychologist

FOOD ADDICTION

Deep fried, loaded with sugar
or grease.
Did I love food, more than
I loved me?
Imagined it, thought about it,
sought it, then ate it.
Became bloated, bloody ill,
constipated—I hate it!
Ate for every imaginable reason,
holiday or not, it was the season.
Happy, sad, stressed, bored,
fiancé just deployed.
Never stopped when I said I would,
just convinced myself that I could.
Chips and candy in my purse
to quench that sweet or crunchy thirst.
Sodas and cookies under the bed,
non-stop strategizing in my head,
anticipating my next sugar fix:
will it be crème brulee, strawberry sorbet,
or dark chocolate pretzel sticks?
Cycle of guilt, shame, and promises
to never overindulge again.
Stopped dieting and drinking tonics.
Ate when hungry and stopped when full.
Rich desserts became the exception,
moderation and movement the rule.

But GOD | 113

"I went to the Lord for help. He answered me and rescued me from all my fears."

Psalm 34:4

"Experts say that eating disorders may affect as many as 7 million young women and a smaller number of men in America today. And sufferers who fall into the trap of thinking they're fat when they're not risk their health and sometimes their lives — to stay that way.

"Step #1. Recognize there is a problem (This can be the hardest part of getting help because eating disorders can be kept secret for years.)

"Step #2. Get help. A combination of prayer, counseling, and behavioral therapy can be effective, although severe cases of anorexia or bulimia may require hospitalization."

—Jeffrey Shicks
Director/National Speaker/Author
Nashville YFC & Reality Check Youth Talks

Freedom Cost

I sleep with the hundreds I killed
when I was on the battlefield.

I returned to my country disabled for life.
Now who will run with my son and dance with my wife?

This body is semi-intact, but my mind is shattered
from bodies of brothers and sisters I could not gather.

You will never know nor recall my name
or recognize that your children's peace flowed through my veins.

My head is held high to have fought for my country of birth.
America is freedom amongst countries on earth.

As you walk your dogs, rest within your homes, and select your coffee or tea,
Remember many are shedding blood around the globe for our Liberty.

"This is how we know what love is: Jesus Christ laid down his life for us. And we ought to lay down our lives for our brothers and sisters."

1 John 3:16

"Oh say can you see?
Home of the Brave.
Land of the free.
'Insure domestic tranquility'

Honor your God, your parents. and family. Honor your country; by doing this, you honor yourself.
Be Courageous, be heard. Speak clearly, speak up for right, speak out against wrong.
Be Committed, promote righteousness, see it through. Whatever you do, do it for the Lord, and He will establish your plans.
My Country, Tis of Thee."

—H. Neail Tyson, USN RET

CHOSEN

Insecure,
so unsure.
But I keep hearing Him say,
"I have chosen you and not cast you away!"
Uncertainty floods my future,
abandonment—a familiar friend.
Neglected by growth hormones
that hair gel can't mend.

Sun rising and setting on hecklers
cause, unlike cheerleaders,
I'm not yet
de ve lop ed.
No curves in my shape,
just pimples
on my "less than perfect" face.
Persistently mocked
about my shoe size and clothes.
Daily questions like,
"Why do you wear the same leggings on top of your hose?"

When asked about dating,
I say, "I can date if I want to,"
though I'd have to be asked out first
for that to be true.

I don't look like the teacher's favorite
or girls chosen as lead in a school drama,
and my peers have never let me live down
the day I overslept and wore pajamas.

But GOD | 117

Dark chocolate skin
with thick lips to frame my grin.
Sure, my family says, "You're so pretty,"
but that's not my reality.

Pressures of being too thin or too fat.
"Why you try to be so proper, why you talk like that?"
(Talk like what?)
"You say 'the' instead of 'da,'
'ask' instead of 'axe.'"

"Do your parents make you talk like dat?"

Not sure I could make it, God,
without daily time with You,
knowing You're there
no matter what I'm going through.

Insecure,
so unsure.
But I believe it when You say,
"You have chosen me and not cast me away!"

> "I took you from the ends of the earth, from its farthest corners I called you. I said, 'You are my servant'; I have chosen you and have not rejected you."
>
> Isaiah 41:9

> "In times of insecurity, doubt, and rejection, we can rest in the arms of a loving God! As you continue your journey, I hope that you would always remember that you are set apart for such a special purpose, and that your full confidence can rest in the truth that you are chosen by our Creator!"

—Chantel Matikke

I See You

Yesterday I locked my door
and turned away my head
when I captured you near the off-ramp
with cardboard sign in hand

This morning I cracked my window
tossing you water and a ham biscuit
When you caught it without flinching
I knew you were just down, not quittin

Friday came and you were not there
You would not release my thoughts.
I stopped after work to purchase dinner.
There you stood   behind the counter

"Whoever is kind to the poor lends to the Lord, and he will reward them for what they have done."

Proverbs 19:17

"Whenever I see a person in need, I am reminded that it could be me. Then I take the time to reflect on how much God has shown me grace and mercy. I used to get volunteers from my team to pass out care packages to those in need every year around the holidays, and it brought us all so much joy. God puts us in positions to be able to bless others regardless of what challenges they are facing. If you can make someone's load lighter, do just that."

—Brittany Renee Williams

A Lie

though spewed
a thousand times
in a thousand
twisted ways
and cuddled by
ten thousand hearts,
is still   untrue
at the end of the day.

"The Lord detests lying lips, but he delights in people who are trustworthy."

Proverbs 12:22

"Lies are bills. Lies are opps. Lies wait patiently from the edge of the world to the edge of your lips. Lies snatch your soul a sentence at a time until the child in you sees a stranger. You can certainly lie your way out of anything, into nothing."

—Martin Tucker
Poet

No Words Necessary

when an elderly neighbor's lawn is teeming with grass,
wild bushes, and debris. I grab hedge shears, garbage bags,
and begin hacking and sacking weeds.

No words necessary

when a father yearns to help his son with homework
but has never learned to read—
you're a gifted reading specialist who just took two year's leave.

No words necessary

when an older woman hugging a sign—
"Will work for food"
and the lunch bag in your backseat has beans and barbeque.

No words necessary

when your classmate's cocker spaniel of ten years
was just put to sleep. You help him create a memory album
of favorite photos he can peruse anytime.

No words necessary
when your hands and feet can speak.

"Dear children, let us not love with words or speech but
with actions and in truth."

I John 3:18

"There is a lot to be said for the familiar phrase, 'Actions Speak Louder Than Words.' Saying 'I love you' can make someone feel special, but after repetition, it tends to become just another familiar phrase. However, actions can speak volumes of love to someone without ever speaking a word. God places opportunities all around us every day. Seek and then act on these opportunities where you can touch another with unspoken love because that kind of love is priceless."

—Michelle Howard

Promises Made

Torn with confusion,
drenched by the illusion
that his drinking would stop.

Years of disappointments,
her tears to anoint them,
until she accepted
that it might not...

Endless hours waiting with hope
trampled by another note
of, "Daddy's sorry, I forgot."

Forgot a promise to attend her Play,
then promises upon promises
to make it up some other way.

"Another way"   that never came
'til the drinking ended
and what remained,

was a daughter's love and unwavering faith
that her daddy would now keep
the promises he made.

"Hope deferred makes the heart sick, But when the desire comes, it is a tree of life."

Proverbs 13:12

"The lives of children are filled with quiet indignities, disappointments of the heart, and compromises of the spirit. They are nothing as dramatic or immediately traumatic as abuse or catastrophe, rather, they are secret injuries of the soul that are accepted and endured. The wonder is not that children can be brought to ground by these injuries. The marvel is the number of children who take flight despite (and sometimes because of) their emotional burdens.

—James Welbourn, Ph. D.
Licensed Therapist

DADDY PRINTS

Daddy prints are all over you,
although you may not know.
Stamped upon your mother's womb
as we watched her belly grow.

Daddy prints were engraved on you
well before then.
It began when your mom and me
became the best of friends!

Bowling, cards, board games,
and a love for great food,
but nothing brought us closer
than your sister and you!

Daddy Prints are all over you, son,
although you may not know.
When you were just a toddler,
where I went, you would go.

Off we went to get a hair cut
or just to the grocery store.
You were my little buddy then,
but today you are much more.

Son, you have my name
and integrity to carry on
to love and respect your mother
even though I am gone.

You may not see me everyday
or hear me say, "I love you, son."
But you were an answer to your
Father's prayers before your life began,

"A father to the fatherless, a defender of widows, is God in his holy dwelling."

Psalm 68:5

"Fatherhood is an awesome privilege and responsibility. 'My Prints' is a tribute to all the fathers, whether deceased or living, who truly love and care for their families. The anticipation of becoming a parent is like no other. Likewise, there is no substitute for spending quality time with our children when we can do so. A real father has enduring love for his children that lives on, even when he is no longer present or alive. May we all take advantage of our opportunity to influence our children while we can."

—Jason Williams

Ditch Digger

"When you do something, do it right the first time"
Dad would say in such a way you knew he meant
it, like "Fetch some eggs for breakfast," or "Turn that television off
and go to bed." Then he'd spew, "Don't make excuses—
make good,"
                         ... and we would.
Like I saw Dad do, I'm up before the sun, replacing tiles
and watering the lawn. He taught me to plant seeds
in a perfectly straight row if you want a pretty yard.
I hear his voice as I trim the sidewalk edges, boxwood hedges,
and reshape the topiary-trees in front of our home of 30 years.
I can't count the times strangers have knocked on my door
to ask, "Who does your landscaping and lawn?"
Their mouths drop when my wife of 52 years says, "My husband.
He is just a man reared by his father to work hard
and do it right the first time."
The electric saw's hum sounds like
Dad's commitment to excellence, especially
when digging ditches in the shoes and britches
he purchased.

> *"**Whatever** you **do**, work at it wholeheartedly as though*
> *you were **doing** it for the **Lord** and not merely for people."*
>
> Colossians 3:23

"Success and motivation in life comes from within. My life has been blessed due to the example set for me by my father. His words of 'do more' and 'be the best' have always echoed in my spirit to accomplish my life's goals. It works! Never settle for less, put forth your best effort because when you do, your work will speak for you!"

—Nathaniel Warren
Retired Dean of Students, Tennis Coach, and
Associate Professor
Norfolk State University

Hollow Throne

Alone, I stood on stage at school,
only strangers there to see.
Took my first leap forward
in hopes that he would be
among the eyes, soon good-byes,
gazing upon me.

Searching, scanning,
still commanding
each twist, turn, and twirl,
but no sign of the one
for me, who shaped my world.

He promised—
But once more, a hollow throne
with father's absent face
would be the forlorn memory
my heart could not erase.

Scripture:

> "I will be a Father to you, and you shall be My sons and daughters, says the LORD Almighty."
>
> II Corinthians 6:18

Just a Thought:

"Children feel sadness and disappointment when a parent is absent from important events in their lives. All children, whether in loving or abusive homes, desire the love, support, and approval of their parents. This need transcends race, gender, culture, and socioeconomic background. When children feel loved and nurtured, they develop self-confidence and feel valued. I strongly urge all parents to take the time to be actively involved in every aspect of your child's life. The memories and modeling behavior you create will forever impact your child's perception of you and influence how they parent their children."

—Barbara S. Mullins, Ed.D.
Professional School Counselor

Why Should I?

Pulled the covers over my head
And sunk back into my bed.
What's the big fuss? Why should I care?
No one even knows I'm there!

Don't need to see anyone.
Don't want to go anyplace.
Just leave me alone.
Get out of my face!

You can't understand
what it's really like.
Worry raids my mind
as I chase sleep at night.

Getting dressed is the great reminder
of how much I detest school,
where I'm ridiculed, rejected,
disrespected, made a fool.

I squirm and sweat when called on
to read or answer a question,
hoping my teacher will call on someone else
When I give her the usual, nothing.

I don't like who I am,
But don't know how to change.
I want good friends and better grades,
So help me   if you can.

"For I know the plans I have for you, declares the Lord, plans to prosper you and not to harm you, plans to give you hope and a future."

Jeremiah 29:11

"Hurting adolescents and teenagers often have negative perceptions of themselves and their world. Parents and educators are in a unique position to influence these children in a positive manner; but we must recognize the opportunity and take advantage of it. It only takes one adult in a school setting to make a difference in a hurting child's life, to let them know that they are valuable."

—Susie Thurman
Educator

BECOMING

From crib to college in lightning speed,
closed my eyes to go to sleep,
woke up and he was as tall as me

Where went the days of cotton soft onesies,
milk-stained bibs, diapers to change,
patting him to sleep, and bottles to fill?

The times when the planet
belonged to him
and his favorite word was "no"
and sharing wasn't a thought until we taught him to.

Where went the days of catching grasshoppers,
chasing rabbits, and climbing trees?
Those days when he cried and ran to Momma
when he fell and scraped his knees?

Tantrums over friends
not following rules of the game.
A problem-solving arsenal
of pouting and calling names.

Where did those days go when his sisters
were banned from his room?
And fun meant galloping around on the broom?

Those days have faded like the height marks
once drawn on the side jambs of his room door.
We now place growth marks for his sons
who are also becoming.

134 | *But GOD*

"Listen, my son, to your father's instruction, and do not forsake your mother's teaching."

Proverbs 1:8

"Two brothers grew up in the same household with loving parents, wanting nothing. Both, as their parents, were active in church; one an usher, the other sang in the choir. One goes on to attend a well-respected University, and the other is serving a two-year sentence on a felony charge. Yet, they are both on a course of 'becoming.' A parent's influence is powerful and limited at the same time. The most powerful weapon we have in helping our children is prayer, prayer, and more prayer. However crooked their road may become at times, we must remember that it is their 'Journey to Becoming.' We, too, are still on our 'Journey of Becoming.' We can be confident that with God's help that both young men still have hope of 'Becoming' all they were created to be!"

—Harold Frelix Jr.

Visit from an Angel

Eyes glued open, wondering how days might differ
if she were here. She'd kiss us, caress us, and pray each night
before dimming the light. All five of us slept in one room
in a queen-size bed like a half dozen donuts sugar-smashed in a box—
minus one

Tonight, I lay in the bottom bunkbed, and goodnights
have become as empty as hot biscuits without butter and jelly.
I tend to miss Momma most between midnight and pre-dawn
when my thoughts of her rise with the silence.

This night was different. Out of a deep slumber, I was awakened
by a brilliant, glowing, Madonna-like figure suspended to the left
of me. My silent screams returned
unanswered. My quivering fingers, toes, and arms were restrained
by an invisible force
unknown to me and never experienced again.

A peaceful presence massaged my muscles and released my breath
to breathe.
I never worried about Momma after that visit—

"For He will command His angels concerning you to
guard you in all your ways."

Psalm 91:11

"In life, we are occasionally confronted with struggles that cause us to flinch, turn back, or become paralyzed. There are even times that we float through a living nightmare. We would be hopeless except that God fortifies us to fear not with a hedge of His mighty angels to fight our battles and to lock us into safe mode. Even a child can rest assured that she is not alone because our Heavenly Father watches over us with loving eyes."

—Chiquita Tucker
Educator/Reading Specialist

Choose Me

One of a billion faces
plastered across wilting pages
desperate for a place to call home.
Years pass, but hope remains steadfast
for parents to call my own.

Never wanting anyone to know
that I was in foster care, so
I pretended my life was "normal,"
kept conversations light and informal

Longing to ask a friend
over to spend the night,
visions of jumping on beds,
bumping and banging our heads,
til forced to turn off the lights

Still waiting, wanting to belong
To a Dad, Mom, sibling of my own.
But assured God has already
that I've not been nor will ever be alone.

"I took you from the ends of the earth, from its farthest corners I called you. I said, You are my servant I have chosen you and have not rejected you."

Isaiah 41:9

"To be cherished, nurtured, and loved is the most desperate heart cry of all mankind, but it is life and breath to a child. Apart from a family, a child will still grow, but it will most always be a halting, weary journey full of the struggle to *become* on his own—what should have been cultivated by a parent. Could there be any higher calling on our lives than to open heart and home to one of these little ones, to receive them as Christ?"

—Sherri Gragg

Thank you for the Dance

You taught me the Harlem Shake and Two-Step
til I could doo-wop through the storm.

We harmonized, "A Change is Coming"
on the back of winters turned warm.

With worn shoes, dull taps, and faded leotard,
I sissone beyond childhood's bittersweet scars

Our sessions orchestrated melodious sounds—
"It's not what happened, but how you respond."

I thank you for the moves and I thank you for the songs
That propelled me to dance above the storm.

Dedicated to Mary Ellen Peterson, Norfolk Virginia, and Ken Graham Nashville TN.

"Surely you need guidance to wage war, and victory is won through many advisers."

Proverbs 24:6

"We often feel that asking for help is a sign of weakness. However, it takes great strength and courage to acknowledge that you need help and to seek that help from someone wiser and more experienced. Whatever you do, don't hesitate to ask for help if what you have tried is not working, or you are just having difficulty coping. Help is often a prayer or phone call away."

—Mrs. Jennifer Matikke MSW

JUST ONE

Just one to listen,
just one to care,
just one to know,
the pain I bare.

Bombarded with teasing,
day in and day out.
"Hey Porky, hey Dumbo,
is that your nose or a snout?"

And this harassment
didn't begin today.
It's been years of torment
and living this way!

Just one to smile at me
when there is no one else
to accept me beyond
this prison called "self."

Just one who will take time
to get to know me inside,
who won't be embarrassed
of sitting beside me at lunch.

Just one kind glance or hello
when I enter or as I go.
To help me get through the day
when kids bully and push me away.

Because they can only see
that I am different from them,
instead of understanding
I, too, am made in the likeness of Him!

"So do not fear, for I am with you; do not be dismayed, for I am your God. I will strengthen you and help you; I will uphold you with my righteous right hand."

Isaiah 41:10

"Our children should truly be the most treasured resource we have. In today's world, we can easily forget how complex a journey can be for our youth. Research tell us that school aged children are among the most at-risk group in our society to be victimized. In the book *Weakfish* by Michael Dorn, we can learn a lot about the teasing and harassment of a child by other children from a child's perspective. I hope that we all become inspired, more than ever, to be "Just One" who is willing to encourage, believe in, and show genuine concern for a child."—

—Pamela Burgess
Educator

LOVED YOU

Loved you through callous-thick rejection.
Offered fervent prayers for your fudge-dipped lies.

Tasted your pain that gushed like a rambutan
as I glimpsed you through the Creator's eyes.

Discounted your sabotage and sniper attacks,
collapsed alongside my fading contempt.

Loved you through tears toppling like boulders,
cleansing unspoken offense.

"Bear with each other and forgive whatever grievances You may have against one another. Forgive as the Lord Forgave you. And over all these +virtues put on love, which binds them all together in perfect unity."

Colossians 3:13-14

"We are all faced with situations at one time or another when others treat us in ways that are very hurtful. These times can be perceived as opportunities to demonstrate the love and forgiveness that is required of Christians. Love is the way we can choose to respond that never fails! Love is the perfect law of liberty that protects us and identifies us with Jesus Christ."

—Lorraine Nwofia
Wife and Mother of five

Come to Me, My Daughter

before you give your heart to my son.
Let Me be your first love,
I long to be that special One—

the One who allows you to see yourself
as you were created to be,
not the world's impression
of your identity.

The only one
who can mirror you,
My daughter, is Me.

Come to Me, My daughter,
I desire to comfort you as no other can.
You will never find
the completion you seek in created man.

Come to Me, My precious daughter,
let Me protect and prepare you for the one
who can only be the man for you
because he first chose to believe in My Son.

Allow Me to make you whole
and fulfill My perfect plan for you.
It is only by knowing Me
that you will come to love and know you.

But GOD | 145

"Daughters of Jerusalem, I charge you by the gazelles and by the does of the field: Do not arouse or awaken love until it so desires."

Song of Solomon 3:5

"In a day and age where girls are forced to grow up too soon and model the behavior they see on TV, where chastity is looked upon as the exception and not the rule, and where character and inner beauty are no longer valued, the message of "Come to Me My Daughter" couldn't be more timely. What a beautiful literary picture of how our Heavenly Father bids every girl and every woman to come to Him for the love, affirmation, and acceptance their hearts desire. Indeed, an intimate relationship with God must precede every relationship so that our sufficiency is found in Christ and not in man. May these words touch your heart and draw you closer to your First Love."

—Hetti-Marie Barroll

Barefoot Republic Camp's

leaders, counselors, and teachers
love the unlovable in us.
They quickly forgive our blunders,
building legs for lasting trust.

Each day was finding a lost flashlight
to navigate our darkness.
Songs awakened sprigs of joy and hope,
diminishing our sorrows.

Barefoot blares of reconciliation to the Cross
and to those who look and live differently than we do.
We ingested truths about the longsuffering
that young Christians must endure.

Days present and days gone, seeds are intentionally sown
through messy games and water sports
that stretch our spirits, souls, and minds,
securing Shepherd's tree roots in hearts
that become our relic of strength over time.

You are our Barnabas and Paul
all rolled into one,
encouraging reconciliation of men
from every nation through the Son!

But GOD | 147

"From one man he made all the nations, that they should inhabit the whole earth; and he marked out their appointed times in history and the boundaries of their lands."

Acts 17:26

"'Barefoot Republic Camp' poignantly reminds us that being barefoot is a sign of vulnerability, our humanity, as well as a sign of our brokenness. It is only when we admit that we are 'barefoot' that we are able to comprehend our need and receive God's provision. God inspires our ministry to serve as a vehicle of hope to an ever-changing society scarred by division, stereotypes, and misunderstanding. Through the gospel of reconciliation, Barefoot offers a glimpse of Heaven to a population of kids in need of the ability to dream of what God can do with their lives by uniting them with their parents, community, and the church to help define His eternal purpose for each one of them."

—Tommy Rhodes
Founder & Executive Director
Barefoot Republic Camp

Pseudo Friends

Pseudo friends,

    so illusive.

        Like time

            they slip away.

Born of our need

    to be accepted and belong,

        we awaken and find

            that as many of our dreams—

                pseudo friends

                    are gone.

"One who has unreliable friends soon comes to ruin, but there is a friend who sticks closer than a brother."

Proverbs 18: 24

"Family and friends are some of the treasures in life that we often take for granted. Our human tendency is to focus on the negative aspects of life, including people in our lives. We see the faults of others so much easier than we see our own. The challenge is to focus on the positive aspects of life and others, recognizing that none of us are perfect."

—Vernae

Today I Started Letting Go

things I couldn't control.
The release of a hundred balloons
I could no longer hold
onto this book
that some said didn't exist
like the kiss you didn't
want to happen
bit it did
Stripped, strained,
Stricken, drained from these balloons
That won't release me,
won't let me fly away.
Popping, splattering spit
won't stop, won't quit
dragging me through fields of daffodils
lined with briar patches
catching, scratching
just enough to relinquish control
of the hundred balloons
I let go.

"Let your eyes look straight ahead, and your eyelids look right before you."

Proverbs 4:25

"Through the grace of God, we can overcome any trial or tribulation at any age. Letting go of attempting to control people, things, and situations is a crucial step in overcoming…"

—Bryan Keith Williams

School

School was more than a brick building
where I said the pledge and prayed;
it was the refuge where I spent
most of my childhood days.

A place where I could laugh
and play, anxiety free.
School was the only place
where I could really be me.

Learning was my great escape
from a home-life I grew to hate.
Our parents worked hard
and were rarely home.
Though the house was full,
I still felt alone.

I tried to fit in with my family
and find a comfortable place,
but it was teachers and friends at school
who accepted and made me feel safe.

"Then people brought little children to Jesus for him to place his hands on them and pray for them. But the disciples rebuked them. Jesus said, 'Let the little children come to me, and do not hinder them, for the kingdom of heaven belongs to such as these.'"

Matthew 19:13-14

"Children come into schools from a multitude of different circumstances. Some come from loving homes, some come from abusive homes. Some come from structure, some from chaos. Some are used to eating three meals a day, others just hope for one. Some love books, as they have been read to since in their mother's womb, while others have never been introduced to a book and the world of imagination. Some are bathed, well rested, and ready for adventure; some are dirty, tired, and just need a hug. Some are emotionally stable; others are very fragile.

Educators have no control over the factors or environments our children are faced with outside the school walls, but we do have an incredible opportunity to level the playing field while they are inside ours. School can be the safe haven for all children; one that provides opportunity, adventure, encouragement, hugs, love, forgiveness, mercy, grace, and hope."

—Debbie Edens
Elementary School Principal

SUMMERS AT BIG MOMMA'S AND GRANDDADDY'S

Summers at Big Momma's and Granddaddy's
were sweeter than ripe peaches fallen to the ground.

Countless hugs, jaws pinched and tugged,
and smiling faces all around

Shopping at farmers markets,
Sunday dinners after church.

Running errands with Big Momma
never felt like work.

Every day was a sunny day
whether the sun was out or not

because for just a little while,
our troubles we forgot.

Sodas and ice cream from Poppa B's,
balloon water fights that left us drenched through our tees.

Rubbing one another's backs
with chilled, watermelon rinds.

Granddaddy yelling from his Cadillac,
"You children had better mind!"

Playing jacks with Sissy, hopscotch, and "Mother may I please?"
while our brothers scouted squirrels and rabbits to tease.

And *mmmmm good!* Big Momma's homemade jellies and jam, fresh fried fish, pickled beets, and deep orange candied yams.

Never a dull moment,
and our spirits were so free

because we knew that Big Momma and Granddaddy
loved us unconditionally!

"I have been reminded of your sincere faith, which first lived in your grandmother Lois and in your mother Eunice, and I am persuaded, now lives in you also."

II Timothy 1:5

"Grandparents play a most important role in the lives of their grandchildren. They are blessed with the opportunity to sow seeds of truth, wisdom, and love that can impact generations. The memories that grandparents create in the hearts and minds of their grandchildren are magical and foster a sense of belonging and self-worth that is priceless. Grandparenting is a gift and privilege, second only to that of parenting. Thank God for Grandparents!"

—Elvester Williams & Kerri Young

THE BUS RIDE

(I)

Fourteen, and my soul was deflated
by my father's displeasure of my lost innocence,
like the well-worn bus seat I sank into.
I had given and lost to an 18-year-old I'd never see again
what my mother had given and lost to Dad. Desperate
to save me from one leviathan
in Atlanta, he inadvertently fed me
to several in Birmingham. I was walking on fragile frays
of chiffon fabric—
ripping the wrong stitch could be fatal.
I loathed the rejection from my father whom I loved.
If only his furrowed brows could have unraveled
like the tootsie roll pop in my pocket
from familiar to familiar; chocolate to chewy chocolate.
Instead, my world was snatched away
like a developing turnip root ripped from the ground—
enough strength to resist the
rocks, worms, and weeds,
but not enough to withstand forced abstraction.

As I gazed out the hazy window
of that giant bus with the painting
of a lean dog, a homeless man lurked outside the bus station,
like my boyfriend's voice, "It will be ok," "It will be ok."
No good-byes, hugs, nor red-rubbed eyes—

A young mother beside me clutched her baby in one arm,
her son in the other—
all Dad tried to hold on to was slipping away
like my departure time. He squeezed me like we'd never
see each other again.
My spirit was the Jumbo flattened Icee cup
in the path of the bus's black tires.

> "The LORD is compassionate and gracious, slow to anger, abounding in love. ⁹ He will not always accuse, nor will he harbor his anger forever."
>
> Psalm103:8-9

> "There are moments in life when we've disappointed others or have been deeply wounded by those closest to us. Many of these actions and consequences, though irreversible, are forgivable. Our response to disappointment is an opportunity to cast shadows or sunshine."
>
> —Vernae

THE BUS RIDE

(II)

The bus seatbelts had the strength of glass noodles
in surviving the thoroughfares to Birmingham.
Every stop with a man trudging off, woman trudging on,
man off, woman on. Bebop, Blues songs
taunted, leaving all I'd ever known behind.
Changing traffic lights, rounding sharp curves
and corners jerked me in and out, out and in
of my father's arms. He had been the sunshine and shade
of my childhood days. Every curve was another obstacle
my four siblings and I would have to navigate without
our mother. The first time apart from one another.
My hope of Dad changing his mind grew wider
with each mile marker on 75 South.
How many discussions had I entertained in disdain
with myself about the moment Dad would discover
I had skipped school to hover with a boy-man?
Would mercy have prevailed over judgment
had his wife, my stepmother of nine years,
not left us again with her daughters, our sisters?
Changing and blinking construction lights signaled
new bed, new school, new schedule, new rules.
The curves cut at every turn as I recall
how promising life had looked just a year earlier. Was I the same
daughter inducted in the National Junior Honor Society
by Yolanda King? The same daughter
who rewrote lyrics to "We've Only Just Begun"
for her 7th grade graduating class to sing?
The same daughter who always wanted to please the father,
whose cracked heart now creaked worse than the bus doors
as they opened for me to   exit   exit   exit.

"Therefore I tell you, do not worry about your life, what you will eat or drink; or about your body, what you will wear. Is not life more than food, and the body more than clothes? Look at the birds of the air; they do not sow or reap or store away in barns, and yet your heavenly Father feeds them. Are you not much more valuable than they? Can any one of you by worrying add a single hour to your life?"

Matthew 6:25-26

"Change can be traumatic for all of us, but especially children and teens, whether forced, warranted, or chosen. We can reassure our children of the constants in their lives and of God's faithfulness to be with us even when our lives take drastic, unexpected turns."

—Vernae

THE BUS RIDE

(III)

No shock, Granddaddy had docked
before the bus reached the depot wearing the exact look
he'd worn while waiting for speckled bass to bite his line—
was   I   the   fish   this time?
Our pupils would meet, greet, and sing
the first stanza of "Amazing Grace"
before he would toss my backpack and suitcase
like a stringer of fish in the trunk of his Cadillac.
The tune of his eyes carried me from death-valley
to a patch of green grass beneath
the magnolia tree in his and Big Mama's front yard.
Less accountability for school was like eating fried fish
without hot sauce—
no one asking to see my homework, report card,
or if I had prepared for tests?
It all smacked me like that catfish's flapping tail
the first time I took it off the hook.
Months of petting and flirting with pot
widened the chasm between me and Christ
and Christ and me.
My guidance counselor
was agave in my kuding cha—
I sipped, I savored, I sifted my past.

My heart would be fresh churned butter
when Dad and his new wife scooped me up
and dropped me at college   three bluegill years later.

160 | *But GOD*

"But because of his great love for us, God, who is rich in mercy, made us alive with Christ even when we were dead in transgressions—it is by grace you have been saved."

Ephesians 2:4-5

"We are privileged to serve a God Who already knows our human frailties and has a plan for our forgiveness and restoration when we look to Him. That plan usually involves others who love us and embrace us when we are still a mess—

just as God loves us when we are still a mess."

—Vernae

This selection is dedicated to the following women who emerged in my high school years and helped me to remember:

Helen Heath, Lydia Meredith, Yvonne Kennedy, Thelma Moore, Marilyn Williamson and Reaver McCall.

REDEMPTION

He Calls

He awakes me gently
between dusk and dawn
to rest within His
omniscient arms.
I go quickly to Him
on the quiet of night
as blackness shrinks
against His light.
I bow my head
and lift my hands,
then wait and watch
for Him to perform
what only He can.
Imparting strength,
wisdom, and joy
He exclusively gives
so that I may learn
to live until   He makes
that final call
     for me to come home
once and for all.

"Be alert and of sober mind. Your enemy the devil prowls around like a roaring lion looking for someone to devour."

Psalm 119:148

"I look forward to my Heavenly Father's calls because I cuddle in His arms to be still and listen to His voice."

—Kay Winslette,
70 years young

Wounded Body

You crucify fellow believers,
seeing them through cynical eyes,
selectively deafening your ears
to muffle   their genuine cries.

You beat them down when broken,
too weak and dejected to stand.
You crush their bloody fingers
as they reach   for your hand.

You fire round upon round
of murderous and contemptuous speech.
You want war in your heart
when they plead   and plead for peace.

You bury your heart of flesh
beneath a heavy heart of stone,
closing doors of unity
where Body members   once belonged.

Have you forgotten the mercy and love
lavished upon you by Jesus Christ?
Have you forgotten how for All your sin,
He became   the final   sacrifice?

"Therefore, as God's chosen people, holy and dearly loved, clothe yourselves with compassion, kindness, humility, gentleness and patience. Bear with each other and forgive one another if any of you has a grievance against someone. Forgive as the Lord forgave you. And over all these virtues put on love, which binds them all together in perfect unity."

Colossians 3:12-14

"How quickly we forget. We are more like the unmerciful servant (Mat. 18) than any of us would want to admit. Apart from the mercy God has shone, each of us would be in line for our own crucifixion. We have each been forgiven so much and at such a great price. What is it again that the Lord requires of us? To act justly and to love mercy and to walk humbly with our God (Mic. 6:8)."

—Pastor Randy Cordell
Lakeshore Christian Church

The Unseen Battle

barged onto my tastebuds
like fresh, crystallized ginger candy. It grabbed
me before I knew I had been grabbed.
I was told that love and justice were also abstract,
yet I smell them, feel them, swallow them—
when innocent men are set free
and neighbors care for an abandoned child
or a widow's eyes still shine
into the evening of her years rolled in tears and laughter.
I was oblivious to things unseen at thirteen.
They weren't clear-cut like working to purchase
Andrae Crouch's album as opposed to stuffing it beneath
my winter coat and walking out of the record shop.
No one explicitly explained that choosing Christ
meant the same as joining the battle of Father Abraham—
the same battle where God would lead him to leave
his country of comfort, battle to take possession
of a strange land, sacrifice Isaac, his miracle-son,
and cast out Ishmael, his first-born.
No warnings that my flesh and spirit
would be in an ongoing tug-of-war
like Essau and Jacob's tussle began
in Rebekah's womb—
"My birthright and blessing."
"No, my birthright and blessing."
I was attacked by a triple braided whip
of the World, my Flesh and Satan—
thrashing me on every side like intense winds
whipping branches from fence to field, field to fence.
The fallen world offering external temporal delights that expedite
Satan's hellions, inciting total rebellion against God—

But GOD | 169

distorting and destroying all God loves.
Worst was my unyielding flesh with its lusts list;
"I want   I want   I want."
Knowledge of this trio
eluded the pages of my public education
and possibly, Education's education.

I now see the unseen battle
as the energy beneath, between, and behind
every visible skirmish striking me through varied faces, places, and times.
Unlike the internal war of my flesh
that can be referenced and owned,
these are inaudible accusations
that stalk me from one place to another, then are gone—
no Body taking ownership for its sniper-like nature.
These obscure enemies
wobble the balance of my balance.
They were there when Rebekah conceived
to deceive Isaac and steal Essau's Blessing.
They stir the untouchable, unlovable atmosphere
of distrust, jealousy, and hate you can't handcuff and incarcerate.
They are those vicious thoughts that kick down your front door
that you promptly chuck out the back.
It is that nodding off and falling asleep
moments after dropping to one's knees to pray.
They became the noose of my night
and the night of my days.

I began to walk closer with God,
and the battles
grew more fierce
for my spirit, body,
and soul as if   nothing
was more crucial than
choosing thoughts.
I would confer command—

170 | *But GOD*

command of my mind,
will, and emotions
that would ultimately drive
my actions and devotion
to the God of Abraham,
Isaac, and Jacob,
Sarah, Rebekah, and Rachel—
imperfect servants who,
if not for God, would have
been overtaken
by our enemies
with invisible bodies.

"The weapons we fight with are not the weapons of the world. On the contrary, they have divine power to demolish strongholds. [5] We demolish arguments and every pretension that sets itself up against the knowledge of God, and we take captive every thought to make it obedient to Christ."

2 Corinthians 10:4-5

"The battle in our minds is not just a conflict to overcome negative thoughts or to offload destructive emotions. We need to have the discipline to let the Truth of God fill our hearts and minds, to form a worldview that helps us extend the Light into the world and not capitulate. The renewing of our minds must be extended to the discipline of thought and learning and training."

—Pastor Allen Jackson
World Outreach Church

SURRENDERED

With failed strength
and broken will,
my penitent heart
now freely yields.

Caustic thoughts
gasping for air
asphyxiate
in grave despair.

Humbled tongue,
abandoned motives,
stripped plans burn
out as votives.

Passions and desires
laid at His feet.
An undisciplined appetite
now retreats.

Familiar spirits
no longer lure
me down a path
that is not pure.

Ego dying,
nothing left
but bare words
and feathered breaths.

Rebellious spirit
collapses to its knees,
seeking only
Him to please.

Thy will be done,
oh Holy One,
my surrendered life
You have won.

> "For whoever desires to save his life will lose it, but whoever loses his life for My sake will find it."
>
> Matthew 16:25

> "Oh, the 'Joy' of full Surrender! Such was the life of Joy Davidson. She found surrendering her unbelief meant finding Christ and <u>finding life eternal</u>. Joy Davidson, in attempting to comfort her husband, C.S. Lewis, as she neared the end of her life of forty-five years in a fight with cancer, requested him to move on beyond her death. Only a surrendered heart could love in this manner."
>
> —Kenny Mauck

Squealing Like an African Cicada

You invite me to the afterwork soiree
and act astonished when I don't fuse
with cells moving opposite my flow—
the flow you know well.
Then you request that I "keep Jesus to a minimum."
Why not just ask me to mask my medulla
like a middle-aged man covers his thinning mane?
Or like you slide framed photos
atop heat stains worn by your mahogany secretariat?
Should I also tuck away my left ventricle
like our grandmother stashed her quintessential cash;
flattened, rolled, and rubber-banned
inside a sock within a can,
neatly squeezed beneath
her brassiere and bloomers?
I'd never request you to dab out your nephrons
as one douses their King Edward Imperial
before entering the house,
then mist their breath to silence the scent
of Old Number Seven.
So let's not stuff our small intestines
into the bloated gut of the never-opened wardrobe,
where piles of unfolded clothes are crammed when guests arrive early.
I'm incapable of lowering the voltage of my volume—
to be the back post of an earring
fallen under the bed during the night,
still muzzled at dawn.
My essence would squeeze through cracks in dark corners
like natural light stretching its arms
wherever it went—
squealing like an African Cicada
until released to destined heights.

174 | *But GOD*

"But whoever denies Me before men, him I will also deny before My Father who is in heaven."

Matthew 10:33

"When I was a young child, I would stare at the record spinning 'round and 'round while listening to the words of my grandmother's favorite song. 'It's just like fii-re, shut up in my bones. Gonna' sing about Jesus, the sweetest story I know!' Those words etched into my soul deeper and deeper every time I heard them. Jeremiah knew that passion and experienced the power. When you've had an encounter with Jesus, you cannot keep Him to yourself!"

—Thomas & Dita Rose
The Rose Factor

Nothing, Yet Everything

I am Nothing,
yet Everything
because I am in Him.
As a sunrise without a sunset,
a leaf without a stem,
so am I without Him.

I am Nothing,
yet Everything
because His Spirit dwells in me.
As a mountain without a rock,
a forest without a tree,
without Him, death
would be my eternal destiny.

I am Nothing,
yet Everything
because I am in Him.
As a river without an ocean,
a treasure chest without gems,
So am I without Him.

"I have been crucified with Christ and I no longer live, but Christ lives in me. The life I now live in the body, I live by faith in the Son of God, who loved me and gave himself for me."

Galatians 2:20

"The beauty of knowing that one is everything in Him sprouts unexplainable assurance. Many of us spend our entire lives attempting to find significance and meaning in something or someone other than ourselves and not the One who created us. It is a very humbling position to recognize that anything that we are, our strengths, gifts, and talents, are all because of Him!"

—Valda Barksdale

More Faithful

More faithful than the sunshine
to escort the morning light;
than an albatross to spread its wings
as it launches into flight.

More faithful than the cedars
to stretch upward toward the sky
and the mother who just gave birth
to discern her infant's cry.

More faithful than the river
to pour into the ocean's mouth.
More faithful than the rain
to relieve the earth from drought.

More faithful than your next breath
and your heart to beat
is God's promise to Believers
who seek refuge beneath His wings.

> "I issue a decree that in every part of my kingdom people must fear and reverence the God of Daniel. For he is the living God and he endures forever. his kingdom will not be destroyed, his dominion will never end."
>
> Daniel 6: 26

"No matter what I must face today, I can face it with 'God confidence' because He provides my every need. He knows what I need before I do. He walks with me daily. Great is His love and faithfulness for His children. What blessed assurance in knowing I don't have to fear the uncertainties of life because God is already there!"

—Sue Ann Cordell
Shine Worthy Lifestyles

WILDFIRE

Spirit of Gossip, hissing, hovering
like clouds before a storm,
infecting one by one with silent lies
that spread faster than an untamed fire.

"You won't believe what I just heard."
"Did you see who he was with?"

Foul feet scamper down scorched hills,
toting tainted tales to eager ears.
The bitter gourd of gossip to one tongue
tastes like agave nectar to another.
Smoky smells of charred character creep
from rock,   to ranch,   to chandelier.
A singeing trail of faux friends
attach to you, seeking higher ground,
then attacking and fleeing when seeing there is none.
Haughty eyes that despise
you for reasons unknown,
yet malicious rumors grow while hearts harden.
Job offers rescinded, invitations stalled,
phone stops ringing, all because truthful lies are deceiving
the gullible and vulnerable,
the educated and sophisticated,
the rude and shrewd.

The same ancient Spirit
hissing, hovering, distorting God's truth
to Eve   that she believed
and then whispered to Adam.
They knew   they were naked   and hid.

180 | *But GOD*

"The tongue of the wise adorns knowledge, but the mouth of the fool gushes folly."

Proverbs 15:2

"The ability to communicate is a gift that we should use wisely. How often do we use our words to hurt, condemn, or in some way taint the character of another? The habit of listening to gossip is just as detrimental as the act of gossip itself. Each of us has the power to use our beautiful voices to speak life, love, and encouragement to one another, but it is a choice."

—Eleanor Williams
Aunt & Friend

Don't Forget to Flush

Don't forget to flush the toilet
after you do your business—
like I've done numerous times
after asking God to forgive me.
I'd lift my face from the floor,
pleading for strength to repent
of repeating that deplorable sin   once more,
still wearing its stench—
didn't wipe, rinse, and wash my hands.
Shoulders slump, throat floating lumps,
head lowered like a dying lily
that wants to live.
Do I question who or what God forgives?
Whether His forgiveness is   enough   enough   enough?
I wipe, I wash, I flush that stuff
before the adversary gets a whiff
of my self-flagellation and condemnation,
reminding me that I still stink;
that my sin makes me ineligible
to serve God
cause my business is still afloat,
staining the Hang Fund Gold commode—

God's forgiveness is final.
I no longer need to marinate
in my sin's odor, study its color,
or measure its length and width.
It is done—
Jesus paid for my sins in full
from birth to death,
in illness and health.
So I flushed the toilet,
repented of my sin,
and started living   like I was forgiven.

182 | *But GOD*

"If we confess our sins, He is faithful and just to forgive us our sins and to cleanse us from all unrighteousness."

I John 1:9

"We all do 'our business' and sin almost daily. We tend to linger in our sins just as some of us linger after emptying our bodies. Truly completing the process of confessing, repentance, and turning away will give us the feeling of contentment. God desires to forgive us fully if we truly don't linger and drag some 'business' away with us."

—Terrie Quick
Dental Hygienist /President Highland Rim Habitat for Humanity

I BELIEVE YOU

I believe YOU over the steel pipe reality
of being homeless, older, female, and black
that confronts my sense of self like each new facial wrinkle and flab.
I Believe YOU.
"My future is better than my past."

I believe YOU more than over-sized hands that
grab more tissue than they need, and need more
tissue than they want others to have.
I Believe YOU.
"Let no one seek his own, but each other's well-being."

I believe YOU over the millions of girls, boys, women, and men
who are stolen, sold, or assaulted annually
for pleasure and greed—
another slave trade.
I Believe YOU.
"Yea, though I walk through the valley
Of the shadow of death, I will fear no evil;
For You are with me; Your rod and Your staff,
they comfort me."

I believe YOU over the statistics
that declare barren futures for hungry,
neglected children who grow up fatherless or motherless
and those abandoned to rear themselves.
I Believe YOU,
are *"A father of the fatherless..."*

184 | *But GOD*

I believe YOU over intrusive thoughts that fire rounds of hollow pointed pessimism to derail belief in YOU, myself, and mankind.

"You are the Christ, the Son of the living God."

*Words in italic are quotes from the Bible.

"Heaven and earth will pass away, but My words will by no means pass away."

Matthew 24:35

"When we believe God over the realities of our life here on earth, we continue to live hoping for a better day, sunshine, mended hearts, and minds, accepting and asking forgiveness. We believe the best for ourselves, our children, grandchildren, family, friends, and those who have wounded us."

—Saundera Crawford
Mother, Grandmother & United States Veteran

THE CROSS

The Cross caresses me with arms of assurance
when I am trembling with fear.

When crushed by rippling rejection,
its voice beckons me near.

Its tender heart permits me to forgive
when I am inclined to coddle resentment.

The Cross' eternal truth grounds me
upon bridges of hope and contentment.

When lured by the lust of my flesh,
I find strength to turn away, focus, and flee

to the foot of the Cross.
There, He provides an unexpected escape for me.

The intersection of the Cross is my conference room
for making life's most arduous decisions.

Its impermeable feet plant me firmly
against this world's insidious illusions.

As my knees grow weak and my hair grows thin,
the Cross remains my source of strength

in a creation whose love has turned cold
toward the aging and innocent.

The Holy Spirit dwells in me through the Cross,
empowering a living faith

that empties my heart of prideful self,
then refills me with its grace.

"God has raised this Jesus to life, and we are all witnesses of it. Therefore, let all Israel be assured of this; God has made this Jesus, whom you crucified, both Lord and Messiah."

Acts 2:32, 36

"At various times in our lives, the toils of life can overwhelm us. And as we search for answers that can comfort the soul, Vernae poignantly reminds us in her poem, "The Cross," that Jesus is always there for us and the cross is our constant symbolic reminder that through Christ we can do all things. 'The Cross' serves as a keepsake that we are not in this by ourselves. This powerful and moving poem reassures us there is still a place of safety from the woes of the world… at *'the cross.'*"

—Carl J. Thomas
Associate Director of Admissions
Berea College

This poem is dedicated to all the Berea College students, like myself, who spent hours at the foot of the cross in William Danforth Chapel.

Worship Him

Has rejection beat you down,
Blow upon Blow upon Blow?
Are you imploding with despair,
no one to call, nowhere to go?

Does all seem lost?
Has pain's pain gone numb?
Are you awaiting something
that may never come?

Worship Him

from the deepest place
man cannot blur nor blind.
It's an inner place, more real
than the steel-toed shoes of time.

"Then he said, 'Lord, I believe!' And he worshiped Him."

John 9:38

"The diagnosis was Parkinson's Disease. Really? Shock! Despair! Self-pity! I did spend a couple of hours by myself in self-pity, asking God 'Why me?' and wondering what my life would be like. Then God whispered, *Why not you! Trust me!* When I can't cut up my food, brush my teeth, wave hello, or write my name, I believe in Him, and **I CAN WORSHIP HIM!**"

—Deby Barnett

THE WHO

Whether you worship with instruments
or quietly and without,
it's not the how, but the *WHO*
that makes your praise devout.

If your preference is to wear lipstick
or nothing on your face,
your outward appearance
factors not in this race.

Whether you sit, stand,
or worship with lifted hands,
it's not the how, but the *WHO*
that transforms and transcends.

If you quote Scripture
with book, chapter, and verse,
neither your memory
nor articulation
secures your eternal worth.

Whether you sing as the angels
or can barely carry a tune,
it's your love, not your talent,
He desires fill every room.

You can have multiple degrees,
a GED, or high school diploma,
intellect and achievements
aren't Master in that moment.

But GOD | 189

Whether you're 72, have stolen or cheated,
God's grace is your sufficient healing.
He cannot fail. He cannot lie.
He is the *WHO* of my worship.

"God is spirit, and those who worship Him must worship in spirit and truth."

John 4:24

"Our culture's obsession with performance and physical appearances has sadly made its way into our churches. Many of us leave our Sunday services feeling 'entertained' rather than more deeply acquainted with our Savior. As we face being overwhelmed with yet another new church program or a multi-million-dollar building campaign, that small voice in our hearts ever reminds us that we worship a God, 'not made with hands'–that it is His Spirit within us that give us life and purpose. May we embrace our relationship with Him above all else."

—Ken Graham
Center for Relational Healing

Beyond Sunday Morning Greetings

Miss Cicely prances
across the sacred threshold
with a radiant smile
and Miss America wave.
Unknown to the jubilant greeters,
shades of depression
color her days.
She labors to rise
from bed before noon,
her phone stares back but rarely calls.
A glimpse of Simeon and her gloom shrinks—
he slogs in with lowered head,
stopping above her waist.
His hands grip Miss Cicely
as she palms
the fretful countenance
on his face.
Simeon's mom
just received a dreadful diagnosis.
Uncertain of what it all means,
the family's reaction leads him to surmise
that it could be worse than it seems.
Miss Cicely consoles him in genuine love,
then offers chocolate, mint, or gum.
Simeon raises his chin. Lip corners curve upward
as he wipes a tear with bare arm.
Glancing back before trotting away, he turns
and asks, "Miss Cicely, you think Mama will be ok?"
"I hope so, only God knows that for sure."
"Just as I Am, Miss Cicely."
"Just as You Are, Simeon"

But GOD | 191

"The righteous cry, and the LORD hears and delivers them out of all of their troubles. The LORD is near to the brokenhearted and saves those who are crushed in spirit."

Psalm 34:17&18

"Unconditional love in relationships is desired beyond the Sunday morning service. In the daily troubles that we all face, there is hope and assurance in Jesus through the Holy Spirit Who enables us to walk in fellowship with God and His people."

—Mrs. Elyssa Rae Garcia

What is the Story of Your Brokenness?

What is the story of your brokenness?
Does it lie lame in grass like a breathless baby bird
whose bill is seen but shall never be heard?

Or is your story like the lone evergreen's
miraculous growth on the lip of the Grand Canyon's wall,
home to the red-tailed hawk's territorial call?

Was your character attacked like a crow massacres
a robin's nestlings, closing beaks and breaking necks?

What   is   the Story   of Your Brokenness?

Were you that de-feathered fowl, twice smacked
on your breast while being stuffed with sage and thyme,
then tossed out in rage because you were overdone?

Did it press pause on your peace like a barn owl's scream
breaks   the night   into bits   robbing your sleep?
Is it for   your children   or   their children that you weep?

What made your tears flood a nameless ocean's crest?
Was it empty tinted bottles that never quenched your thirst?
Or the arms of a stranger who became your curse?

Was it the vicious assault on your veracity as a cassowary slices a predator,
so desperate to fight back, speak out, and defend   your name,
yet knowing   in silence   your strength remained.

Whatever the story of your brokenness,
be blind, be barren, be the bird with broken bone—
the now and next moments are the moments you can own.

But GOD | 193

"He heals the brokenhearted and binds up their wounds."

Psalm 147:3

"This written open confession of life's desperateness and cruel disposition is a deep, heart wrenching realization of the human condition. The memories of one's brokenness is the fodder of depression and despair. The invitation is to examine your brokenness and then choose to transcend the hopelessness of your reality or past. Whatever the story of your brokenness, hope and peace await you through a relationship with Jesus Christ."

—Paul Huseby

FORGIVEN

The Cross
is a
powerful
s y m b o l
of the Blood JESUS shed for us all.
He was falsely accused, murdered, and abused,
so our sins
could be
f o r g i v e n.

"And He died for all, that those who live should no longer live for themselves, but for Him who died for them and rose again."

II Corinthians 5:15

"Oh, how we seem to push our anger aside instead of being a forgiven person. Let us forgive the wrong done to us; it is best to be the forgiven one as we move forward in life, instead of holding on to the problem that is festering like a pimple in our heart, waiting to pop."

—Jane Chrisman
Administrative Assistant

LOVE COVERS

when eternal things are forsaken
for pleasures that will not last.
When man wants to remind
you of failures from your past.

Love covers

when people treat you like you are guilty
but have only a smidgeon of fact.
When your character is grossly distorted,
your testimony undermined and attacked.

Love covers

when you are taken for granted,
disrespected, and abused.
When you try to do what is right,
yet are still falsely accused.

Love covers

when your rolling tears of joy
are recounted as tears of guilt and sorrow.
When today's sun is so dark,
you want to forego yesterday's tomorrow.

Love covers

at the day's end
when you lay down, close your eyes,
and choose to still love.

"Above all, love each other deeply, because love covers over a multitude of sins."

I Peter 4:8

"Life is not always fair. When directed at us the insensitive evil acts of men tend to destroy our faith in ourselves as well as others. While we cannot change others or our own past behavior, we can let God's love and forgiveness shine through us. He can help us change our reactions to others. God loves us unconditionally, with fidelity and purity, no matter what others may think of us. As we strive to be more Christ-like in our own behavior, His love will cover us."

—Peggy Thigpen
Retired Lead School Psychologist

WHAT A JOY

To soak in His presence
is to know Him more.
Bowed before His Holiness
Who we exalt and adore.

Sentinel of my heart and mind
when perfect plans go wrong,
with a reassuring word
or the solace of a song.

To lie at Father's feet
is to rest within His arms,
feel completion in His love,
and seek refuge from all harm.

The One Who delivers me
when I open a door to sin
and protects me from dangers
that destroy from within.

What a joy to know
whatever the day may bring,
It can be laid before our Lord
Who is faithful in all things.

"You make known to me the path of life; you will fill me with joy in your presence, with eternal pleasures at your right hand."

Psalm 16:11

"This life is full of pleasures, people, things, and experiences that make us feel happy. However, none can compare to the infinite joy that we can experience when we are in relationship with Christ Jesus. Each day, we can live in freedom and victory because of the joy that freely flows from Christ to us. His joy will always sustain us, unlike the quickly fading happiness that we experience from the pleasures in this life that are based on people and circumstances."

—Vernae

The Great "I AM"

carves mountains
into the chambers of man's heart,
deeper than the Mariana Trench.

He is a dream giver
and a thought sifter.
He is a situation changer
and a promotion arranger.
He is a game maker
and an addiction breaker.

The Great I AM is a just Ruler
and a Temper Cooler.
He is a Truth Illuminator
and a Gossip Eliminator.

He is a Divorce Rate Slicer
and a Marriage Spicer.
He is an Evil Exterminator
and a Curse Eradicator.

The Great I AM opens doors
that were ABUS granit-locked and closed.
He warms souls that were Oymyakon cold
and transforms yesterday's scum into tomorrow's top gun.
He heals the sick and humbles the rich.
He strengthens the weak and makes the dull quick.
God levels the playing field for the orphan and impoverished,
hearing pleas of the humble and forgotten.
He brings calmness to chaos and joy to despair.

He is the Great "I Am".

"God said to Moses, "I AM WHO I AM. This is what you are to say to the Israelites: I AM has sent me to you."

Exodus 3:14

"God can do the impossible. HE has no equal."

—Anonymous

COMFORT LESS

No one,
no thing,
can ever bring
me comfort
like You.

No touch,
no crutch,
means
as much

as my hope
of being
with You.

"Praise be to the God and Father of our Lord Jesus Christ, the Father of compassion and the God of all comfort."

II Corinthians 1:3

"There are times in this life when we are so overwhelmed by grief that it is only our hope of a future time with God that provides any measure of comfort. This is not a desire for death, but for a life void of the pain we are experiencing at that moment or in that season. Knowing the difference can save your life."

—Vernae

In Every Moment

I wipe night from my eyes
and inhale the day's first breath.
I could not see You,
but like the breeze,
I knew You were there.

In Every Moment
Blind-sided by the oncologist report—
stage four melanoma at my door,
banging with a hickory stick.
I answer quickly with fasting and prayer,
confident you would be there.

In Every Moment
Incessant arguing with my spouse's
contentious spirit for years,
averse to yielding to unity and reason,
leaving our home broken and bleeding,
but we continued to love and live
because You were there.

In Every Moment
Children hungry, bills due
while an over-burdened husband
strikes out at you.
A complaining wife
destroying her home
with an untamed tongue,
but both remained strong
knowing You were there.

But GOD | 203

In Every Moment
Dehydrated tears drench
family lesions once denied.
Unshattered by truth and trial,
You were our silk thread knots
in a strand of cultured pearls—
there, holding us together.

In Every Moment

"Even there your hand will guide me, your right hand will hold me fast."

Psalm 139:10

"God created time and space, and we live in one extremely tiny speck of His vast creation. When we are at our best and celebrating, God is with us. When we are at our worst and the situations around us have caused inexpressible pain, He is with us. When we have caused pain in the lives of others and moved away from what God has asked of us, He has not moved and is still with us. He is omnipresent. He was there in our past; He is in our present; He is waiting for us in our future. On our deathbed, He is already there with us."

—Kevin Mckechnie, M.D.

WORSHIP THEE

Thoughts of You
release my praise
for the sacrificial
love You gave.

Bowed head,
bended knees
as I enter in
to worship Thee.

Melodies spring forth
from my mind,
then flood my heart
with the Divine.

You fill me with
Your love and peace
that consumes my spirit
as I worship Thee!

"Let everything that has breath praise the LORD. Praise the LORD!"

Psalm 150:6

"Our hearts are made to worship—they are made to praise our Creator. But so often, our affections are captured by other things, and we worship the created and the evil instead of our good Father. We prefer to gaze at ourselves than at the beauty of Christ. We build up our kingdoms of comfort and reputation, and so we become twisted. But God, in His grace, can call us back and show us our deep need of Him. He covers us with Christ and calls us beautiful until our hard hearts soften, and we cry, 'Glory!' as we were created to do."

—Gabrielle Pryor

BE STILL AND KNOW

Stop fretting child.
Go back to sleep.
Rest your worries
within My peace.
Stop that wringing
of your hands.
Remember the Rock
upon which you stand.
This battle may seem
insurmountable too,
but recall the wars
I've won for you.
Victory is unattainable
in your human strength.
That is why this battle
is not yours, but HIS.
Be still and know
whatever your situation,
however great your opposition,
God is forever faithful
and permanently positioned
to deliver you.

"Have I not commanded you? Be strong and of good courage; do not be afraid, nor be dismayed, for the Lord your God is with you wherever you go."

Joshua 1:9

"We busy ourselves in life and forget the debt that Jesus paid, as well as the power and authority God has given us through Christ to overcome the trouble of this world. We can find contentment in being still and knowing that He is God over any problem we may encounter in this life."

—Mrs. Tamika Jolly
United States Army Veteran

THE ANSWER

When my bones become weary
from clocking in and clocking out,
putting uniform on, taking it off—
the Answer is my purpose,
my goal, my time to hold.

When my feet are blistered and swollen
from dusting trophies, cleaning toilets and tubs,
the Answer then becomes
my royal resting hub.

The day's worry pounds
like giant raindrops
racing from clouds to spore to ground.
From Him, in Him, and through Him,
my Answer can be found.

My husband is on the phone,
a grandson tugs me to hear his new roar.
The Answer's grace is sufficient,
and my less is suddenly more.

My Answer was conceived miraculously
and lived a life without sin.
He plopped upon me like those giant raindrops—
I, too, opened myself, and He entered in.

But GOD | 209

"Jesus answered, 'I am the way, and the truth and the life. No one comes to the Father except through me.'"

John 14:6

"Yes, Jesus *is* the answer to any of life's problems. Unfortunately, Satan deceives mankind into expecting instant gratification and pleasure in all aspects of life to feel 'problem free' and 'happy.'

As Christians mature (at any age), they begin to realize that Jesus never promised us a life of luxury, nor one free of worries. In fact, He said, 'In this world you <u>will have trouble</u>.' (John 16:33). Your relationship with Jesus will not guarantee absence of problems; it *will* provide the ability to cope with life's problems."

—Walter Rouse

Words From My Barber

Plopped down in his chair for a haircut,
whining about my honey's habits,
housekeeping, and lavish life.
Tough truths began to flow from my Barber—
I tore home to apologize to my wife.

Our son earned a "D" in chemistry,
and worse yet, he hid it from me.
The razor hushed as my baritone Barber spoke
"Your son's grade and integrity can recover,
but should his father's words become his yoke?"

Layoffs soon became my norm,
leaving me worthlessly torn
over how to provide for my family.
My Barber said, "I know our families depend on us,
but remember Who you can trust. God is faithful
to meet our needs even during layoffs."

Weeks later I dropped in to get my beard shaped,
discouraged, dejected, and broke;
when familiar laughter among boys and men
edged me from despair into hope—

But GOD | 211

"Whatever you do, work at it with all your heart, as working for the Lord, not for human masters, since you know that you will receive an inheritance from the Lord as a reward. It is the Lord Christ you are serving."

Colossians 3:23-24

"Barbershops are places men and women go to get more than a haircut. It can be a place of rich conversation that invites reflection, peace, and perspective."

—Anonymous

THE WALK

begins climbing a gravel-paved road.
I spot a tainted penny
and pocket it beside a perfectly polished quarter.
I press onward to greener charted paths,
through a scourge of mosquitos and fire ants.
A silver-crowned couple strolls
opposite my side of the road—
lips and hips locked like the sweat to my brow.
I cross over and declare,
"Hello. Beware, lest this day spoils you both."
They blush and resume blooming.
A whiff of sweet honeycrisp apples and tart limes intertwine,
beckoning me to pause at the farmer's market.
I grab a bunch of tender turnip greens for Sunday dinner—
to discover my money declined the walk.
The cashier kindly whispers,
"I'll guard your greens until you return."
Marching past a one-story brick house for sale,
I smile and wave to potential buyers
entering and exiting like rabbits, their warren.
My neighbor, Carmen, paces the sidewalk
in front of her home like the scented fruit roaming
the farmer's market, anxious to be bought and bitten.

Spring has arrived without her husband of 45 years—
their hips and lips no longer lock.
A half-pony from my porch, I glance up at the glistening white cross
adorning the church pinnacle across the street,
like a star atop a Christmas tree.

But GOD | 213

My walk was neither glistening, white, nor bare—
It dripped red like juices from the cherries and tomatoes
waiting alongside my greens at the farmer's market.
Reaching deep inside my pocket to retrieve the tarnished penny,
I unearth a plain-edged glossy copper coin—
three-fourth of an inch in diameter.

I wonder how Carmen's life will transform
as she commences her new walk?

"Dear friends, since God so loved us, we also ought to love one another."

I John 4:11

"My husband was a timid man who kept to himself and rarely talked about his affections. What a gift to hear stories of your husband's love for you from neighbors you barely knew and lived just a few feet away. Neighbors who came to know and love you through your husband's walks, talks, and waves over the years. His daily walk was an example of the Savior he came to know and love throughout our marriage. His kindness toward our neighbors and theirs toward him cost nothing."

—Carmen Seward

BONUS POEMS FOR YOUR PRESCHOOLERS

IF I WERE REAL

If I were real, I would lap water
with my long, thick, slobbering tongue.
I would chase squirrels and rabbits from bush to tree all day long.

If I were real, I would stop and sniff everything in sight
and leave my scent on every bush
from morning to moonlight.

If I were real, I would scratch
my itches everywhere,
beneath my long floppy ears
and short silky hair.

If I were real, I would eat
table food every single day
and hide the yucky dog food that is usually thrown away.

If I were real, I would lie on my back
for soothing tummy rubs
and wag my tail like a windshield wiper whenever I got hugs.
If only I were   real

"Now faith is confidence in what we hope for and assurance about what we do not see."

Hebrews 11:1

But GOD | 217

"At some point in time, every child longs for a pet. The child longs for it so badly that imagining every detail of the animal comes to life in the mind. For some, the details come true."

—Anonymous

Teddy Wet My Bed

Oh no! Hey, wake up Teddy,
You wet my bed again!
Our pajamas are soaked
all the way to the sheets.

You must have been dreaming
you were in the bathroom
instead of in bed with me.

I told you not to drink water
before we went to bed.
Shh! But Teddy is stuffed with foam,
so he didn't hear a word I said.

Let's get up and change our pajamas
and make us a tent on the floor.
Teddy, please use the bathroom before bed,
or you can't sleep with me anymore.

> "For in him all things were created: things in heaven and on earth, visible and invisible, whether thrones or powers or rulers or authorities; all things have been created through him and for him."
>
> Colossians 3:13

"What holds us tighter than sleep? Perhaps determination. Even though I was potty trained decades ago, there are nights when sleep's insistence can suppress my bladder's stretch. And then there was my young daughter, who willed her bladder shut while busy with daytime play. As her mood escalated, we'd suggest... request... demand she relieve us all. Our powers were small against her mighty will."

—Mary Craig
Mom

Where are Your Manners

Where are your manners?
Wherever have they gone?
Did you say you left
"Yes, please," and "Thank you" at home?

And what happened to "Excuse me"?
It's so nice when he's around.
Why, when you bumped right into me,
he was nowhere to be found.

Best go back home to get them
very soon and right away
because your best dressed manners
will be needed everyday.

"Teach them to your children, talking about them when you sit at home and when you walk along the road, when you lie down and when you get up."

Deuteronomy 11:19

"Simple, sweet words, easy to understand. In a hurry, go-go world, many of us have stopped using our manners that were taught to us as children. The phrase 'do unto others' has been forgotten. My parents expected us to have good manners. By doing so, it reflected pride to our parents as having taught us well. Children learn by watching what we as adults do. These sweet words do not take time away from our daily activities."

—Mrs. Faye Painter

But GOD | 221

Bubbles

   Bubbles   floating
beneath cotton-candy skies,
   leaping over puffs and ponytails
of children skipping by.
   Drifting through ripe pumpkin patches
of soon to be pumpkin pies.
   Why do the bubbles fall and burst
right before our eyes?

Jesus said, "Let the little children come to me, and do not hinder them, for the kingdom of heaven belongs to such as these."

                Matthew 19:14

"A bubble can be representative of the innocence of children. Bubbles float 'innocently' until they pop. In thinking about children, we understand that they are born innocently into the world. They are socialized by parental figures attitudes and beliefs. Faith in what we are taught shapes who we are as people. We must rely on our faith to conceptualize our experiences. Throughout development, we depend on our faith to protect us from harm."

                —Anonymous

Just Being Me

I colored on the kitchen floor
and glued giraffes on the walls.
I tried to paint the ceilings,
but my legs were not that tall.

I put lotion in my curly hair
so I would look like Dad,
instead, it got all in my ears
and just made Mommy mad.

I pulled leaves off the plants inside
that looked just like the weeds
Mommy pulls from her garden
before she plants new seeds.

I filled the big boy potty
with a nice new roll of tissue.
Grandma smiled at me and said,
"Whatever will we do with you?"

"For You formed my inwards parts; You covered me in my mother's womb."

Psalm 139:13

But GOD

"Every child is unique in their own special way. The difference in my daughters is what made them uniquely them, and this is true for every child. Their uniqueness may be tough to appreciate at times. However, they were made for a purpose, and their uniqueness is how they will fulfill their purpose."

—Misty Edde
Wife, Mother, and Special Ed. Teacher

Kind Lady

Kind Lady, Kind Lady, I'm hungry
and really want to eat.
Kind Lady, would you nurse me
with your milk so sweet?

Kind Lady, Kind Lady, I'm wet,
and my diaper needs to be changed.
Would you put me on a clean one
so that I can be dry again?

Kind Lady, Kind Lady,
would you sing me the song
that you and the Kind man
like to dance to and hum?

Kind Lady, Kind Lady, my gums itch.
Please rub them and hold me tight
until the Kind man comes home
and rocks me to sleep tonight.

"Her children rise up and call her blessed; her husband also and he praises her."

Proverbs 31:28

But GOD

"A mother's love can never be replaced. As a child grows and learns to be independent, they still fall to their mother's arms in times of need. That need may change from bottles and diapers to homework and recipes. The one thing that never changes are the prayers that have been prayed and the lasting love that 'Kind Lady' continues to give."

—Marie Ray
Children's Ministry

THANK YOU

Thank you for my eyes.
Thank you for my cheeks.
Thank you for my nose
and how you created me!

Thank you for my skin
that keeps me warm within.
Thank you for my smile
that wiggles when I grin!

Thank you for my tiny toes
and for my tiny feet.
Thank you for the arms
that hold me as I fall asleep.

"Before I formed you in the womb I knew[a] you, before you were born I set you apart; I appointed you as a prophet to the nations."

Jeremiah 1:5

"It is such a huge blessing as a mother to watch my children pray. As they fold their little hands and bow their little heads, I am quickly reminded of how simple and innocent their prayers are. Many times, adults are so distracted by the world that they miss all the blessings that children see, such as Popsicles, rain, swimming, birthday cake, and toys, just to name a few. I always knew it was very important for me to teach my children to be thankful, but in return, they have taught me to take a break from being a responsible adult and see the world through their eyes."

—Kayla Cook,
A Thankful Mother of Two

BUTTERFLY

Butterfly on a leaf,

wearing colors just like me

black, orange with popcorn white,

now it's flying past the kite.

It just landed on my favorite tree.

    I see the butterfly,

        but can it see me?

"For by him all things were created, in heaven and on earth, visible and invisible, whether thrones or dominions or rulers or authorities—all things were created through him and for him."

Colossians 1:16

"God made so many beautiful things for us to see! The butterfly has so many colors on its wings. God took time creating each animal to look just the way He wanted. God created you too! He made you special, so there is no one else like you. God takes care of the butterfly, and He takes care of you. God made you, and He loves you so much that He made butterflies!"

—Mrs. Heather Crawford
Wife and Mother of Two

"Momma Said"

Momma said, "Go to bed,"
but I wanted to stay up.
Momma said, "Take a sip,"
but I drank the whole big cup.

Momma said, "Come inside now,"
but I wanted to stay out.
Momma said, "Give me a hug,"
but I refused and began to pout.

Momma said, "Pick up your toys,"
but I still wanted to play.
Then Momma gave me "the look"
and said, "You must learn to obey."

"Children, obey your parents in everything, for this pleases the Lord."

Colossians 3:20

"Sometimes, it's hard to make good choices. It's hard to always obey. But the Bible tells us that God wants us to obey all the time. 'Obey' means to follow directions, even when you don't want to. Mommy and Daddy need you to obey so that you can be safe and happy. When you listen to Mommy and Daddy and follow their directions, you will make them very happy. But, most important, you will make God very happy!"

—Amy Thomas
Wife & Mother

Poor Fly

That fly is trying
to taste my honey.
Its wings are stuck,
and it's not funny.

Tugging, togging to break free
from that sticky blob of honey.

I want to help the fly
but what can I do?
Maybe I can wash off the sweet honey
like I do when my fingers
are stuck together with glue.

Poor fly.
That did not work.

"Teach them to your children, talking about them when you sit at home and when you walk along the road, when you lie down and when you get up."

Deuteronomy 11:19

"Children can be taught kindness and concern at a very young age… for others, themselves, and even for a fly. Kindness is not to be taken lightly, for every day, it is lost. Teach your children to be kind to others. You never know when kindness is the help someone really needs."

—Edward Henry
Highschool Student

Where's My Lunch

When I opened up
my big box of lunch,
my favorite foods
were not inside to munch

No turkey sandwich
with pickles and cheese.
What are these tiny green
bush-like trees?

No chips to be found,
only crunchy white things
with seeds in the middle
and green skin all around!

And where is my chewy
chocolate chip cookie?
Someone took my mom
or she is playing hooky!

"He said to them, 'When you pray, say: Father, hallowed be your name, your kingdom come. Give us each day our daily bread.'"

Luke 11: 2-3

"God has given us our bodies to take care of while we are here on earth. One of the most basic ways to take good care of our bodies is by making sure we eat a healthy diet. Our children learn from us how important this is, and by starting early, healthy eating has life-long benefits. We do not have to be a famous chef with a lot of extra time to feed our children well balanced, healthy diets."

—Mike and Becky Schwartz
Children & Youth Ministry

Sleepy **T**ime

Angelic face with sleepy eyes,
puckered lips and blooming cheeks,
nestled in his comfy bed
ready now to sleep.

Bottom pointing to the stars,
knees curled into his chest,
hands folded beneath his chin,
ready now to rest.

A gentle kiss to his forehead
as not to stir the peace
of our darling little blessing
who has fallen fast asleep.

"In vain you rise early and stay up late, toiling for food to eat for he grants sleep to[a] those he loves."

Psalm 127:2

"One of my favorite things to do is sleep. It helps your body and your brain. Many things happen while you sleep. Your body gets to rest from all the play that you did today. You gain energy for all the things you want to do tomorrow. You can even grow while you are asleep. God watches over you as you sleep. It makes me feel safe to know that God is with me always. I can't wait to see what tomorrow brings."

—Tracy Hall,
Wife and Mother

Mother's Love

I saw her face first every morning
when I awoke from sleep.
She'd whisper, *Good morning, Pumpkin Lumpkin,*
while tickling my feet!

She would dress me and comb my hair,
then feed me cream of wheat.
But not before we thanked God
for the breakfast we would eat!

She has the kindest eyes
that I have ever seen.
Her voice made my heart flutter
like her sewing machine.

She would hug me and cuddle me
like a perfect gift from above.
Even my favorite blanket
doesn't warm me like my mother's love—
that I will never forget.

"Keep your lives free from the love of money and be content with what you have, because God has said, Never will I leave you; never will I forsake you."

Hebrews 13:5

"One of the earliest memories I have of my mother was somewhere near twenty-nine years ago. While she was getting me and my sister dressed for the day, others were hurrying to get to church nearby. The beautiful church bells swept me far away from that small room with its white-washed walls, metal beds, and bare floors. Living without her would be a tough road for me and my three siblings. She spent somewhere around seventeen years battling addictions and abuse and living out of sight from the rest of the world. Birthdays were especially hard. I always wondered if she ever thought of me, remembering the day I was born into her world. The people of Israel wondered the same thing in Isaiah 49:15. They felt forgotten, lost, and abandoned. But Christ promised that He would never leave us or forsake us. In that verse, He vows that He will never forget you, and that He has engraved you into the psalms of His hands. Trust Him, and believe in His promises. If you have been separated from a parent, know that God has an amazing plan for you, and that you were hand chosen by the one and only true God."

—Dita Rose
Wife and Mother of Two

Toddler's Response to Newborn Sister

Look, she's out of Mommy's tummy!
Is there another baby in there?
Why is she so little?
Look at her feet
and her hands.
They are way smaller than mine.
Daddy, will she stay little or grow big like me?
Oh no! Her teeth are all gone!
Daddy, where are our baby's teeth?
She is just crying.
Can she talk to me?
How can I talk to her if she can't talk?
Can she walk?
But I want to play with her now!
Mommy, please can you make her play with me?
Babies can't do anything.
She cannot even feed herself.
But it's ok, baby sister, I will take care of you.

"But Jesus said, 'Let the little children come to me and do not hinder them, for to such belongs the kingdom of heaven.'"

Matthew 19:14

"A young child is so inquisitive and innocent. They naturally ask questions and say things based on their perceptions of the world that is usually quite different from us as parents."

—Quasia Walker

No

I say *No*
because it is easy,
and when I say it,
big people stop
and look at me.
Some look angry,
others puzzled or amused.
I usually say it again
cause it seems like
they expect me to.
There is something
powerful about *No*.
It makes me feel
a bit of control
over something in
my small new world;
a world that takes me daily
for a tumble or twirl.
It makes me feel bigger,
like I can make choices,
however tiny
they may be.
Saying *No* to big people
is my way of becoming
a more confident little me!

"For the promise is to you and to your children, and to all who are afar off, as many as the Lord our God will call."

Acts 2:39

"Saying 'no' is the beginning of our children's long road to independence and, prayerfully, obedience. May we have wisdom as parents to respond to 'no' in a loving way that sets clear boundaries, high expectations, and provides healthy choices that support obedience and independence in our growing children."

—Vernae

Jesus Watches Over Me

Jesus watches over me
when I'm good
and when I'm bad.
Jesus watches over me
when I'm happy
and when I'm sad.
Jesus watches over me
when I'm awake
and when I'm sleep.
Jesus watches over me
every day of the week.
Jesus watches over me
just like He watches over you.
Jesus Christ, He loves me
and He loves you too!

"For the Lord watches over the way of the righteous, but the way of the wicked leads to destruction."

Psalm 1:6

"It is good to know that Jesus watches over us all the time. Even when we think no one else sees us, He is still watching. When we obey His teachings, He protects and guides us. Even when we disobey, He still loves us and continues to call us near to Him."

—Ayriel Coffee
Wife and Mother of two

Sleep Training

What is going on?
Don't you hear
your darling screaming?

Just pick me up,
and I will hush
and get back to my dreaming.

You know,
I could be teething
or soaking wet?

And all this crying
is making your precious
sweat.

Crying always led
to you picking me up before.
Don't you want me to be happy anymore?

Whose bright idea was it
to let me lie here and scream
until I cried myself to sleep?

It may be great for
mommy's and daddy's,
but could someone tell them
it is not working out for me.

"A woman giving birth to a child has pain because her time has come; but when her baby is born she forgets the anguish because of her joy that a child is born into the world."

John 16:21

"Some people say to sleep with your children so they feel loved and secure. Some people say to let your children cry themselves to sleep so they learn how to calm themselves. Times change, and so do opinions. Learn to trust yourself as the mother of your children. When what you do for children is done with love, it will be right for your family. You will figure it out together."

—Peggy Lucas
Wife, Mother, and 3rd Grade Teacher

TIME TO RISE

The sun's peeping through
the window in my room.
Mom says, "It's time to rise,"
but I think it's much too soon.

I squeeze my eyes,
pretending to be asleep.
But mom's too quiet,
so I take a peek.

There she stands, eyes glued to me. "Time to Rise
if you want to see
what kind of day
it is going to be!"

> "Arise, shine, for your light has come, and the glory of the LORD rises upon you."
>
> Isaiah 60:1

> "As parents, we sometimes forget that our children are like every other child in the world. They want our love and affection first thing. They are not concerned with making sure that everything goes completely right so they can get somewhere on time. In their eyes, they don't see time, schedules, or deadlines. They see their parent/s every morning, pulling their covers back to start a new day. They depend on and look forward to our hugs, kisses, and 'I Love You.'"
>
> —Reshonder Holmes
> Mom

www.ingramcontent.com/pod-product-compliance
Lightning Source LLC
Chambersburg PA
CBHW072106201224
19346CB00004B/56